CONSENT CODES

A MODERN FRAMEWORK FOR SEX, POWER, AND DIGNITY

STEF HAMMETT

CONSENT CODES

Publisher: HMS Publishing

https://www.havemore.space/

Author's Contact

To book the author to speak at your next event or to order bulk copies of this book, please, use the information below:

hello@havemore.space

Printed in the United States of America.

CONTENTS

INTRODUCTION

AN OPERATOR'S MANUAL FOR SEXUAL SAFETY

"Your power lies somewhere between immobilization or being a puppet pulled by someone else's strings..."
Stephen R. Covey's "The 7 Habits of Highly Effective People: Powerful Lessons In Personal Change."

I welcome you to the pages of a book that does not necessarily seek to teach you anything new, but to encourage you to engage in critical thought about issues you are already familiar with, and perhaps to arrive at your own conclusions on how to navigate new *codes* and *concepts* that you will encounter in the book. But first, allow me to introduce myself. For all practical purposes, I am such a commonly encountered woman in society that I might easily pass for your sister, your mom, your friend, or someone you met at a bar. As you encounter me here, you may feel a certain sense of *déjà vu*; that strange, fleeting feeling that you and I have met before, even though you know you haven't. You simply can't place me. But that is only because I'm no different from you.

I am a woman who has thrived in large ecosystems—geographical, cultural, and professional—across America and overseas. My work and passions have taken me across industries, cultures, and communities—from boardrooms to intimate coaching conversations—giving me a wide perspective on where safety breaks down and where it thrives.

Perhaps most importantly for this book, I'm a woman who genuinely loves men. I love all kinds of men in all the appropriate ways. I express my love for men through deep listening, empathy, respect for boundaries, and fostering genuine emotional intimacy by often meeting men exactly where they are, a key business principle. For me, these are consistent behaviors that demonstrate the love, care, and partnership that lead to mutual growth and respect. It is because of this fundamental mindset about men that I am capable of noticing, appreciating, and cherishing when environments feel safe for everyone, and I am unrepentantly passionate about creating those spaces.

Ultimately, my mission here is to create the space for change, and that change is for a new operating system that can provide safety for the evolution of highly sexually evolved communities. I believe that today's empowered world is one in which we have better-connected communities, enhanced care for the individual, and the technology to enable anyone to live on their own terms, or on the terms they prefer in their relationships with others. Today's society can afford a zero-tolerance policy for environments in which women feel unsafe, especially within US borders.

WHAT IS THIS BOOK ALL ABOUT?

This book is about turning *kind of human* into *human kindness*. To avoid confusion, let me differentiate between the two. *Kind of human* classifies or describes our nature. For instance, we might say, *That is a strange kind of human behavior,* or *We are all the same kind of human.* Therefore, it groups us based on our shared characteristics that define what makes us human. *Human kindness,* on the other hand, describes the *quality* of showing respect, awareness, and grace to others, stemming from our shared humanity. It often goes beyond being superficially nice, with "kindness" representing a deep, courageous choice to help. To clarify, we are all the *same kind of human,* but true *human kindness* is an active choice to embody the best of that humanity through the compassionate actions we display towards each other every day. By acknowledging the difference between the two, this book outlines the codes I can identify whenever and wherever safety is compromised, especially for women.

The framework is simple: three commands. Delete code. Edit code. Save code. Apply them to our communities, culture, and connections—and human kindness becomes the default setting. In other words, it taps into our inherent capacity for compassionate, selfless, and considerate behavior towards each other as soon as we truly recognize our shared connection. That is why, for all practical purposes, this book serves as a manual from an *operator* who advocates for a core operating system for humanity, fully acknowledging that, unfortunately, humanity's current operating system is riddled with malware in the form of a fundamental disrespect for the basic tenets that bind our humanity together. Coming from a background of decision-making that has led to genuine corporate scalability, operational clarity, and cross-functional team building in many companies, I bring my own intuitive insight to create a space for those ripples of meaningful change that can reconcile our age-old conflicts.

To cut out the rot in the system, we must strike at the root of the problem. The root of the problem is our old operating system. Indeed, the pervasive rot in our society stems from being burdened with an outdated operating system. Yet, this isn't necessarily an *internal* flaw. Rather, an *external* systemic force is responsible for the malware, simply because the source code has been infected. A cursory look at society today reveals that many people are prone to irrational impulses and decisions largely driven by primeval fear and insecurity. The only way we can create space for safety is by addressing these fears and insecurities. For anyone who agrees that this problem actually exists but doesn't know what to do about it, this book provides actionable steps. It will teach you to *teach* differently, *coach* differently, and *engage* differently.

WHY I DECIDED TO WRITE THIS BOOK

I have already mentioned the malware that we are grappling with. I worked on many personal cases involving these issues and was confronted with a *confused* and *confusing* system riddled with that malware—one that costs a surprising amount of both time and money to navigate. My options felt like a simple decision: *I could ignore it and appear negligent, or I could respond, creating a potential for my words to be weaponized.* Fortunately, my abundance mindset came to my rescue. The question then *became, Why don't you write a book about the systemic negligence fueled by capitalism and supported by the patriarchal rules we are all familiar with?* I am not saying anything that is not already public knowledge; if you look for it or connect enough dots, these details are found across Netflix, podcasts, governmental documents, and everywhere. I am simply providing you with ideas for codes to help you understand and navigate. This book seeks to examine the operating system across communities in the United States, identify the old system, clarify the malware, and provide concepts to create the much more beautiful world we all know is possible (as illustrated by Charles Eisenstein).

WHAT IS MY AIM HERE?

My aim is to help you achieve clarity about the choices life presents you with. You gain greater power when you have clarity regarding your desires and what those desires will accept or condone. This clarity comes with far greater ease for some, while for others, it is earned the hard way. Traumatic incidents create a larger gap on the path to gaining such clarity. Sometimes, the point of trauma creates new patterns, especially if the trauma is of a sexual nature. This lack of clarity is more damaging to minds that are still too young and perhaps too vulnerable and impressionable to understand what they desire or why they even desire it in the first place. That is why different codes are needed, and these codes are alluded to in Stephen R. Covey's *The 7 Habits of Highly Effective People: Powerful Lessons In Personal Change*. The First Habit in that book, *Be Proactive*, discusses a critical code for safety: understanding our center and its four core elements: *wisdom, security, guidance,* and *power.* In that section of his book, Stephen Covey also offers a powerful quote: "Your power lies somewhere between immobilization or being a puppet pulled by someone else's strings..."

This delicate concept, proposed by one of the most intriguing minds of our time, highlights the contrast between inaction—*immobilization*—and being controlled by others—*a puppet pulled by someone else's strings.* Covey's valid argument is that real power comes from *proactivity*, which is the ability to act according to one's own values and influence one's own life rather than being passively influenced by external circumstances and other people. This proactive approach is central to his first habit, *Be Proactive.*

More than any other country on Earth, the United States has historically spent enormous sums of taxpayer money on the defense of our shores. Yet, the very notion of safety itself is at risk all over the land, especially for women, and specifically for those with vulnerable identities. What we have is either an instinctual fear-based narrative or one that is firmly ingrained in one's consciousness by society. The narrative takes the form of seemingly thoughtful warnings that are actually and subtly designed to shift the blame from aggressors to victims. "You ought to know better than to go down that road. You shouldn't have walked down that street all by yourself. How could you have been on such a dangerous trail all alone? You shouldn't have traveled alone. How could you have gone to that house? Decent girls are never found hanging out at that bar." The very existence of this *shift-the-blame* narrative stems from a patriarchally programmed notion that is historically rooted in some degree of truth. Admittedly, there was indeed a time when it was necessary for a woman to be accompanied by a man for her safety to be guaranteed. In fact, this may even have nothing to do with being male or female, but simply with perceived human vulnerability in a brutal and uncertain era.

One can also understand the need to be protected from wild animals while traversing a jungle terrain or the need to be cautious while traveling in areas where strangers might be viewed as threats. But, in this day and age, we cannot restrict individual safety to such a narrow corridor of consideration. It misguidedly suffocates women with exaggerated yet unnecessary concern, suggesting that their very existence alone is inherently unsafe and in need of protection. The old, flawed system is crippling human interaction and safety.

The violators of human safety come in all forms: male, female, short, tall, in power, and under power. There are super simple *human-to-human codes* that articulate kindness and showcase how those who never witnessed kindness while growing up can reprogram themselves for a much safer world. *Let's recall an understanding that hurt people hurt people.* Essentially, this means that individuals who have experienced trauma or deep emotional wounds are often inclined to replicate unkind and harmful behaviors in their own lives, inflicting pain or trauma on others and creating a cycle of hurt. Naturally, this occurs because their own unhealed wounds propel them into defensiveness, leading them to lash out or act in self-protective ways that harm those close to them. I am not on a mission to excuse those hurtful actions, but merely to offer an explanation for that pattern of behavior.

It is important to emphasize that not all hurt people hurt others; some may even become more empathetic as a result of their past experiences. For the purpose of this discussion, however, you might find tools necessary to be present in a space where you can help people who are in need of healing. One fact is undeniable: *healing overcomes hurt,* and that gives us one code that can truly re-empower human-to-human kindness. This book was not written to tele-guide you. It was written in the hope that perhaps you will learn something; perhaps you will question something, and maybe you will recognize a situation in your own life that will make you ask the question, *Can I code it better?*

WHAT WILL YOU TAKE AWAY FROM THIS BOOK?

It is important that you understand that this entire narrative comes from an aggregation of experiences. In-depth research into individual stories and specific cases allows us to highlight the nuanced human interactions that create the space for certain, very vital conversations. *What are those conversations?* They are the hard discussions we must have if we are to ultimately achieve the sexual safety that will ensure our world can thrive better on a platform of mutual respect and kindness between the sexes. Again, that is why this book is also a *manual* of sorts. It is a *manual* from an *operator* who understands that consent isn't a mere buzzword. In this manual, you will find practical codes to navigate differently, and to teach, coach, and engage with greater clarity. You will cultivate the ability to know when to say *yes* and when to say *no* without hurting anyone. Ultimately, you are being given a lens through which you will be able to see the world moving toward *human kindness* rather than staying stuck in *kind of human.*

WHO ARE YOU, THE READER OF THIS BOOK?

You could be anyone from a broad range of people. You could be someone working in or with experience in the sexual assault space. You could be a parent trying to help your teenager understand the complex issue of sexual assault. You may be a teacher seeking greater knowledge to share with your students. You may be a business leader who wants to understand the problem and explore how you can contribute to a safer environment. To you, the empowered women who want to learn how to support others, and to you, the fathers who need more knowledge on how to explain this to your kids, I say welcome to a book that will serve as both an *eye opener* and a *space opener* for greater safety in our communities.

CHAPTER ONE
THE SOURCE CODE

Using Codes To Compel Behavioral Change

"Be ruthless with systems, be kind with people."
Michael Brooks
Chanel Contos (Teach Us Consent founder)

One Word Is the First Problem: A Source Code Called The Sheath

For any trend to take root, there is always a *source code*, and in our society, that source code is language. This language is expressed in one word; just one word. That word is *"sheath."* This indicates that the source code of our societal dilemma is *sheath.* If we are going to fix the glitch, we must examine the source code. *Why is language so powerful?* Language is powerful because it is the fundamental tool for human connection. It shapes our thoughts, cultures, identities, and societies by allowing us to share ideas, build relationships, pass down knowledge, and influence perceptions, with the ability to both unite and divide, build up and tear down, and even challenge existing power structures. Language shapes how we think. It also shapes how and what we remember, and how we perceive reality, thereby influencing our decisions and actions. Language carries our unique histories, traditions, and values, ultimately defining our cultural identity by allowing our heritage to be passed down. In fact, losing our language often means losing our culture. Language derives its power from the vehicle of the spoken and written word. Yet, it is also powerful because of the ideas and emotions that are embedded in, and implied by, those words.

One particular word has shaped how medicine, law, and culture have understood the female body since the 1680s. The word is *vagina.* The term "vagina" comes from the Latin word for "sheath" or "scabbard," the holder for a sword. Thus, the connotation is quite simple. The female body has, for many practical purposes, been named solely by its function to "hold" the male organ. The female body has not been given the privilege to be its *own thing.* It is merely an accessory. It is a parking spot. This is not just ancient trivia. This has consistently been the code underlying whatever perception women have been accorded over the centuries. And it's still in effect. In 2020, a study of 2,000 American women found that nearly 25% couldn't correctly identify the vagina on a diagram of their own body. Three hundred years of medical terminology, and we still confuse the word we use every day with the parts it doesn't even describe. That code has a price tag.

When the language itself frames women as the casing for the weapon, should we be surprised when the system doesn't know how to treat them? No. Women are done being the "accessory" to the "weapon" — especially when they are the source from which the weapon came in the first place. That's why we consistently challenge the medieval connotation of the vagina to arrive at something different: empowerment. A perspective that celebrates a woman's control over her own body and sexuality. One where she can feel confident and unapologetic about sexual choices driven by healthy, intrinsic desires — rooted in a sense of feminine divinity.

THE $122,461 RECEIPT

What is the cost of non-consensual behavior in the United States? The Centers for Disease Control (CDC) estimated a $3.1 trillion lifetime economic burden in 2014 dollars. Adjusted for today? Over $4 trillion — and counting. To grasp matters in stark contrast, let us zoom in to the individual level. From the CDC's Special Report by researchers Peterson, DeGue, Florence, and Lokey titled, *"Lifetime Economic Burden of Rape Among U.S. Adults"* (2017), published in the American Journal of Preventive Medicine 52(6):691-701, we gather that non-consensual behavior actually costs $122,461 per victim. Let us break down the researchers' findings. Based on data, more than 25 million U.S. adults have been raped. This estimate included $1.2 trillion (39% of the total) in medical costs; $1.6 trillion (52%) in lost work productivity among victims and perpetrators; $234 billion (8%) in criminal justice activities; and $36 billion (1%) in other costs, including victim property loss or damage. Note that government sources pay an estimated $1 trillion (32%) of this lifetime economic burden. This is not just pain and suffering; it translates to nothing short of staggering economic loss wrapped in lost productivity, huge medical bills, and a massive toll on the criminal justice system. When you sum all this across the 25 million Americans who have experienced rape, you arrive at $3.1 trillion, a third of which is paid by the American government. Since the government is intended for the people by the people, that means the money is paid by us.

That is why *consent* is not a soft topic. It is a line item we're all funding, whether we choose to talk about it or not. Now, let's get serious for a moment. So, what is the cost of running this faulty code? In business, when a system fails, we look at the P&L. We look at the bottom line. Let's cut out the commercials and get down to brass tacks. The bottom line of our current consent culture is bankrupting us. To tax someone, beyond its commonly acknowledged definition of a compulsory contribution to state revenue, is to demand, drain, or impose a heavy burden on that person's energy and resources, requiring significant effort to address.

In this context, the term implies something that is wearing, strenuous, or exhausting, pushing that person's limits mentally or physically. We are being taxed heavily for the wrong code. We are paying for a system that refuses to update its security software. That is the cost of all the lost productivity, the medical bills, and the legal fees. The bottom line is simply that non-consensual behavior is a public tax.

FAULTY DESIGN, FAULTY CODING

The standard crash test dummy used by the National Highway Traffic Safety Administration (NHTSA) for its five-star safety ratings was developed in 1978, modeled after a 5-foot-9, 171-pound man. Now look at the "female" version. That female version is a smaller male dummy with a rubber jacket to represent breasts, routinely tested in the passenger or back seat — seldom in the driver's seat, even though the majority of licensed drivers are women. The statistics tell a brutal story.

Women are 73% more likely to be seriously injured in a frontal collision. Women are 17% more likely to die in a comparable crash (2022 NHTSA). A 2024 Duke University study found that younger women are approximately 20% more likely to suffer a fatal injury than a man of the same age — regardless of seating position, airbag deployment, or seatbelt use. The system wasn't built with malice. It was built with a design flaw, and that flaw has a body count. Although the November 2025 update is that the U.S. Transportation Department has approved specifications for the THOR-05F, a new female crash test dummy designed to better reflect anatomical differences, its implementation is by no means guaranteed.

The safety systems meant to protect human life were literally designed for a specific *type* of human body, and if you didn't fit that reference, the system wasn't built for you. This creates a hardware incompatibility that has become a life-or-death issue. The argument here is not about blaming the engineers who designed the crash test dummy in 1978. It is more about recognizing that when you build a system based on only half the population, the other half ends up paying the price. My reference to the *Reference Man* in the standard crash test dummy seeks relevance in its application to something much more intimate than a sedan: the female body, its safety, and the code we've all been programmed to follow since birth. To put it more clearly, the same mindset that is responsible for the design flaw in the crash test dummy is also present in society's flawed coding regarding sexual safety, leaving women at the mercy of that faulty programming.

THE INVERTED PENIS THEORY

For over a thousand years, medical physiology operated on Galen's *one-sex model.* Galen, or more formally, Galen of Pergamon, was a Greek physician, surgeon, and philosopher. Considered one of the most accomplished medical researchers of his era, Galen influenced the development of anatomy, physiology, and pathology, with his views dominating Western medicine for more than 1,300 years. In his groundbreaking book, *Making Sex: Body and Gender from the Greeks to* Freud, Thomas Laqueur describes the *one-sex* theory, which refers to the belief that there was only one sex and it was male. This theory originated in Galen's writings, where he suggested a structural homology between the sexual organs of men and women, asserting that they were fundamentally the same, except that those of men lay outside the body while those of women lay inside. In other words, they were reversed, with a vagina being a penis turned inside out, while the ovaries were analogous to testicles. The difference between men and women, therefore, was not one of kind—two fundamentally different types of beings—but one of degree: variations of the same being. The theory held that, in the final stages of gestation, immediately preceding birth, heat caused the sexual organs to develop outside the fetus's body and create a male. However, if there was not enough heat, an incompletely formed male—meaning a female—would be born. Thus, this model posited that females were actually imperfectly formed males, leading to all the social and cultural consequences that followed, including exclusion from higher spiritual, political, or intellectual positions in society. Naturally, it also prescribed subservience and obedience to their male counterparts, along with severe restrictions in legal and economic matters.

There is an interesting corollary to the theory. If a girl reaches puberty and sufficient heat is applied, she could force her sexual organs out of her body and become a *boy*. Believe it or not, the sixteenth century actually offers accounts attesting to such transformations. For instance, the story told by a certain Antoine Loqueneux attributes such a change to the *heat of passion;* a girl in bed with a chambermaid becomes so sexually aroused that she suddenly ejects a male member from her body and continues her life and sexual activity as a male. In all these instances, I suppose we are being vastly entertained by both the sublime and the ridiculous. Thomas Laqueur, in his book, suggests that Galen's theory was the fundamental operative model for understanding sex and sexuality, not only in the Renaissance but even as far as the eighteenth century. Although in his equally important book, *A Woman Down to Her Bones: The Anatomy of Sexual Difference in the Sixteenth and Early Seventeenth Centuries*, Michael Stolberg debunks and argues strongly against it, the seed had already been firmly sown in the consciousness of a gullible world that women were simply *inside-out men*, with the vagina as an interior penis and the ovaries as testicles that did not drop due to inadequate heat. When all is said and done, the female body wasn't seen as different; it was viewed as defective at worst, or incomplete at best. That was the code that persisted for centuries. The interesting thing is that the flawed code didn't simply disappear when science evolved into a field that proposed more credible and provable theories. It went underground to become a subterranean concept that remained in society's consciousness. Society's dilemma is very clear. When we build systems around the 'Reference Man' and define women as the 'Sheath,' we create a culture where boundaries become blurred—because accessories aren't supposed to have boundaries. They're simply meant to be available.

WHO IS ACTUALLY AT RISK?

One in five women will be raped in her lifetime. One in four women will experience severe physical violence from an intimate partner. These figures are backed by empirical data. Based on statistical information from the Centers for

Disease Control and Prevention (CDC) and the National Institute of Justice, and according to the CDC's National Intimate Partner and Sexual Violence Survey (NISVS), one in five women (about 21.3%) in the United States have experienced actual or attempted rape during their lifetime, and nearly half of all women (about 43.6%) have experienced some form of contact sexual violence during their lifetime, including rape, sexual coercion, and unwanted or unsolicited sexual contact. These figures are consistent across multiple studies and are considered a reasonably accurate average, despite researchers believing that the actual prevalence is likely underestimated due to underreporting caused by shame, stigma, or fear, or a combination of the three.

However, those are not the figures that should stop you in your tracks. The statistic that should truly capture your attention is that girls between the ages of 16 to 19 are four times more likely than the general population to experience sexual violence. *Four times!* According to the Centers for Disease Control and Prevention (CDC), these assailants are not hooded strangers in alleyways. Ninety-three percent of juvenile victims knew their perpetrators, with 59% being acquaintances, 34% being family, and only 7% being strangers. The danger isn't out there. It is right here in the family living room. It is lurking behind wine glasses at the party. It is a familiar face and a familiar voice. In agriculture, it is well known that the insect eating the leafy green has taken residence right on the vegetable itself.

CONSENT IS NOT A CONTRACT

There's a kindergarten class in Wisconsin where kids choose how they want to be greeted each morning: a hug, a high five, a handshake, a fist bump, or a wave. The only rule? Honor every classmate's choice. No forced affection. No "hug your uncle" programming. Each child shows up as a community member while remaining the CEO of her own body. That's the new code, and it starts at five years old. But what exactly are we teaching them?

The word *consent* is derived from the Latin verb *consentire*, which literally means *to feel together*. That Latin root itself is composed of two parts: *con*, meaning "with" or "together," and *sentire*, meaning "to feel," "to perceive," or "to sense." While the literal Latin meaning is "to feel together" or "to share feelings," the modern English meaning is "agreeing, giving permission," or voluntarily accepting what is proposed. Essentially, it means not agreeing under pressure; to *feel together*. Consent isn't is a shared sensation. As soon as we treat consent like a checkbox, we have already lost the plot.

While asking for the checkbox can sometimes be a first step, understanding what the word actually means is very important. In our everyday understanding of the word, consent is permission for something to happen or agreement to do something. Affirmative consent relies on "yes means yes" rather than "no means no." If that is the case, then consent must be seen to rest on *three* pillars: The first is *Knowing*. Consent is an active process of willingly, knowingly, and freely choosing to participate in sex of any kind with another person. The second is *Voluntary*. Consent demands informed, voluntary, honest, and mutual agreement. It is ongoing and must be asked for at every step of the way. Let's get intimate here. If you want to move to the next level of intimacy, ask. Consent can be withdrawn at any time, and consenting to one sexual activity does not automatically mean consenting to another sexual activity. The third is *Mutual*. Consent must be seen as a shared responsibility. It is mutually given or affirmed when there is an invitation to sex, and the answer on everyone's part should be a clear and unambiguous *Yes*.

Consent can be given verbally or non-verbally, as long as those words or actions clearly communicate a willingness to engage in the sexual activity. Assumptions are dangerous. As soon as there is confusion or ambiguity, participants need to pause and discuss their mutual willingness to continue. Fundamentally, consent requires communication, and that means, in a sexual relationship, it is about communicating your own interest, listening to your partner's interest, and moving ahead with sexual activity only if you both agree. From the foregoing, it goes without saying that manipulated or coerced sexual activity is not consensual, and silence or lack of resistance does not indicate consent.

FLIPPING THE SWITCH FROM SHEATH TO SOVEREIGN

In conclusion, I'm not sharing this to cause disquiet or discomfort. I don't wallow in problems; I fix workflows. The goal of this book, and the movement behind it, is to rewrite the code — to move from a definition of "sheath," an accessory to be filled, to a definition of "consent," whose etymology is simply beautiful: from con (together) and sentire (to feel), literally meaning "to feel together."

Consent is not a contract signed in triplicate. It's not a legal disclaimer. It is a shared sensation — a moment in which two human beings agree to exist in the same reality, with the same enthusiasm.

I don't harbor resentment or hatred toward the "sword." I love men. I appreciate the energy they bring to our shared humanity and our shared sexuality. My mission is to raise awareness that the "scabbard" is not an inanimate object. It is a person. An individual with feelings and emotions. More importantly, it is a sovereign territory — with its own borders, its own right to self-governance, its own economy, and its own right to say, "Not today!"

Women are done being crash test dummies in the passenger seat. It's time to design a safety rating that actually works for everyone. We've been beta-testing humanity like a glitchy app. The time has come for Version 2.0 with better user consent.

Welcome to the systems upgrade — one that re-empowers the feminine and re-energizes the masculine for a more responsible approach to female autonomy. Ultimately, we are on a mission to transform "Kind of Human" to "Human Kindness."

CHAPTER TWO

THE PROTECTION CODE

Rigging The Zip Code Lottery

"ZIP Code may not be destiny, but it's as hard to fight as gravity." — Jay Wamsted. Title of a May 15, 2020 article by a high school Math teacher

The facts will make you uncomfortable. Scott Galloway, professor at NYU Stern and business expert, puts it bluntly in *The Algebra of Happiness: Notes on the Pursuit of Success, Love, and Meaning.* Your trajectory is largely set before you even start driving a car. By age 30, your income is predicted less by grit and hustle, and more by two factors — your university pedigree and the zip code where you work.

Raj Chetty's data makes it undeniable. He is a highly influential economist at Harvard University, renowned for his data-driven research on economic mobility, equality of opportunity, and public policy. His *Opportunity Atlas* answers a crucial question: *Which neighborhoods in America offer children the best chance to rise out of poverty?* The Opportunity Atlas tracks 20 million Americans and shows that moving a child from a below-average neighborhood to an above-average one — sometimes just a few miles away — increases their lifetime earnings by roughly $200,000. The numbers are from a specific place and time — but the pattern they reveal is not. A Harvard/Census Bureau study found that 44% of Black men from low-income families in Watts were incarcerated, compared to 6.2% in Compton — 2.3 miles away. Same city. Different zip code. Different fate.

But here's where the economic data misses the somatic reality. The fight-or-flight response is your body's automatic, survival-driven reaction to a perceived threat, activating the sympathetic nervous system to prepare you to either fight the danger or flee from it. You cannot execute the algebra of success if your internal operating system is stuck in fight-or-flight. We measure "generational wealth" in assets, real estate, and trust funds. But the most valuable asset a child can inherit is a regulated nervous system—one not left at the mercy of threats that relentlessly activate it until she becomes a psychological wreck.

Safety is the ultimate liquidity. It's the only currency that allows a human being to stop scanning for threats and start investing in their future.

DADS NETWORK

The time has come to talk about Dads. I am under no illusion that this might prove a sensitive subject to some. However, let us look at the numbers again. The *Safe Dad* isn't just a metaphor; it is a statistical firewall against trauma. Research confirms that maltreatment is lowest among children who live with two biological parents. Conversely, studies confirm that a father's presence is positively correlated with a daughter's resilience and her ability to respond to risk. When a daughter feels protected; when she has that "secure base," the tendency is for her to explore the world differently. Certainly, she doesn't walk into a room timidly apologizing for her existence. She walks in knowing she has a formidable support system. Have you heard about the Dad who escorts his daughter outside through the front door to meet her first date for the first time? Such a Dad is sending three messages to his daughter's date: she has a formidable support system, she is valued by her parents, and the daughter's date is being held accountable.

Protective fathers embody tremendous power. That is why fathers of daughters constitute the largest untapped network for consent culture change. They already understand the stakes involved, as their concern for their daughters is deep and visceral. My mission acknowledges and honors that instinct while providing a framework for channeling it. According to the *U.S. Census Bureau Data (2022-2024); Fatherhood Commission; Pew Research Center*, there are 72 million fathers in the United States, constituting approximately 55% of men aged 16 and over with at least one biological child of any age. The total number of children under 18 in the United States is about 73 million, and roughly half are daughters. Fifty-seven percent of fathers consider parenthood extremely important to their identity. A 2024 *Frontiers in Psychology Study* found that father presence positively correlated with daughters' resilience, meaning their ability to respond to risks and challenges. Fathers tend to be psychological security mediators, providing daughters with feelings of warmth, safety, and support. A significant quote from that study states, "Active parental engagement from the father as a primary attachment figure enables the daughter to fulfill her fundamental psychological needs through this relationship, contributing to many aspects of her life, such as resilience in responding to risks and challenges."

SKIN SUIT AND ENERGY

Skin Suit: The body you're walking around in. Male or female hardware. **Energy:** The operating system underneath. Masculine or feminine—and everyone runs both.

Not everyone reading these words will have that *Safe Dad,* and some women may find themselves, as single moms, carrying the burden of multiple roles. This isn't about shame, nor is it about feelings of inadequacy or failure. What we aim to do here is identify a missing energy source so that we can replicate it. We need to distinguish between the *Skin Suit* and the *Energy.*

We all walk around in a *Skin Suit* .Mine is female, while my neighbor's might be male. This is nothing more than the hardware we use to interact with the world. Underneath the Skin Suit, however, we are running operating systems composed of *energies,* of which there are two types. The Masculine Energy is structural, protective, and action-oriented. The Feminine Energy, on the other hand, is intuitive, receptive, and flow-oriented. Now, here is the pivotal truth: the *Safe Dad* data proves that *Protective Energy* is the firewall, the barrier installed to prevent the spread of the *fire of exploitation.* Historically, we have consistently outsourced much of the job of protection to the Male Skin Suit. Yet, if the entire truth be told, protection is a function and not a gender role. In our mission to establish the Protective Energy Code, we will be turning convention on its head because what we need are not more biological fathers. What we need are more humans, regardless of their Skin Suit, who are willing to run the Protective Energy Code. The single mother carrying the weight of ten people? She's already doing it. The uncle who shows up every Saturday? He's doing it. The coach who makes sure every kid gets home safe? He's doing it. Protection is a function. Step into it.

THE VILLAGE FIREWALL

The problem isn't that we have *bad apples.* The problem is that we are running a *bad operating system.* We have designed a society that relies entirely on the *Nuclear Family* to generate the protective energy a child needs. This design is fatally flawed because it creates a single, unalterable point of failure. If that unit, the *Nuclear Family,* fractures—through divorce, death, or dysfunction—the entire fabric of the safety zip code collapses. *What is the cost?* There are two types: the *financial cost* and the *emotional cost.* The financial cost is staggering. The financial cost of divorce to the U.S. economy is estimated at $33B+ from direct legal expenses, lost productivity, and significant drops in post-divorce income, particularly for women, impacting everything from individual wealth to corporate profits through decreased worker output and increased social support needs. In fact, at the very individual level, *Forbes Finance Council* in an October 20, 2022 article by *Tyler Lang, CFA*, estimated the average cost of a divorce to be $15,000 per person and can even increase to $100,000 for more complicated situations, such as a custody dispute. Yet, even these seemingly enormous figures pale in comparison to the emotional cost: the *safety zip code* can take years to repair.

That is why we need a better architecture. We need a *Village Firewall.* And it turns out, we're evolutionarily designed for exactly that. Anthropologist and primatologist Dr. Sarah Blaffer Hrdy is a professor emerita at the University of California, Davis. In her groundbreaking book, *_Mothers and Others - The Evolutionary Origins of Mutual Understanding*, she argues that humans are cooperative breeders because raising our uniquely helpless, long-dependent children requires help from many non-parental caregivers, or *allomothers*, a system that is crucial for survival, fostering empathy, and enabling those cognitive leaps that define humanity.

A key aspect of her argument is that non-biological caregivers, like fathers, grandmothers, siblings, or other community members, whom she calls *alloparents*, became essential, sharing feeding and nurturing duties. Her thesis counters the *sex contract* model in which the father provides while the mother nurtures, by showing that shared care was more important. Her message is clear: we literally couldn't have survived as a species without "alloparents," people other than the mother or father who helped raise the child. Instructively, in hunter-gatherer societies, infants had up to 10-15 caregivers. Today, we try to accomplish the same feat with two caregivers, and sometimes only one.

Nothing could be more unsustainable. We need to shift our thinking from *One-to-One*, one father protecting one child, to *One-to-Many*, a community protecting the child. In fact, in many African societies, the concept of a community raising a child is often encapsulated by the Swahili term *Ubuntu*, which roughly translates to *I am because we are*, emphasizing the interconnectedness of humanity.

This philosophy is expressed in the common African phrase, "it takes a village to raise a child," and key aspects of this concept include the collective responsibility that ensures child-rearing is not solely the responsibility of the biological parents. The entire community—extended family, neighbors, elders, and friends—shares the duty of nurturing and disciplining the child.

We all know the person referred to as the *Office Mom*. He might be a guy named Dave in the accounting department, but he fills the "Mom" function, ensuring that the tribe remains cohesive. The *Community Dad* is that single person operating in high-functioning Protective Energy mode, securing the entire community. This is the selfless coach who teaches about boundaries, not just layups. This is the uncle who keeps watch over the entire block. Ultimately, the question isn't, *Do you have a father?* The more pertinent and absolutely vital question is, *Do you have access to the protective function?*

BUILDING THE CODE

We have to stop waiting. Stop waiting for the *perfect family* to save us. Stop waiting for some heroic man in a specific skin suit to show up and lock the doors.

Here's the shift: We are the infrastructure.

We can build the *Safety Zip Code* wherever we are. The code is portable—we carry it in how we show up, how we hold boundaries, and how we refuse to let predatory behavior slide in our presence. When you consciously embody Protective Energy, you're not just protecting yourself; you're actively recreating the *High Opportunity Zip Code* for everyone around you.

We are all civil engineers. We have the skills to build bridges of safety between each other. The tragedy is that we've been using those same skills to erect walls instead.

This is the shift from *Kind of Human* to *Human Kindness*.

Kind of Human looks away. It assumes safety is a private matter—someone else's problem, someone else's zip code.

Human Kindness looks outward. It recognizes that my regulated nervous system can help regulate yours. It understands that protection is a shared asset, not a scarce resource.

When we build a culture where the Protective Function is abundant, the people we love can finally lower their shoulders. They can stop scanning for threats. They can stop surviving and start living.

That is the Protection Code.

CHAPTER THREE

DEFINING THE CONSENT CODE

Deleting The Bad Code and Replacing It With Community Care

"If we wish to preserve a free society, it is essential that we recognize that the desirability of a particular object is not sufficient justification for the use of coercion."
Friedrich August von Hayek

If you work in any modern environment, you will come across "CC" every single day. CC connotes *Carbon Copy*. Carbon Copy originated from the use of carbon paper for duplicates. The concept is now used in emails to send a copy to others for their information and to keep them in the loop. Having become a trait that is now firmly ingrained in our subconscious programming, it's become a default setting—a habit we replicate reflexively because the workflow dictates it. The fundamental thesis of this chapter is that the "CC" isn't just in your digital communications. It is the hidden code that runs pervasively throughout your entire life. We are currently operating on a cultural software update that is not just decades outdated but also riddled with glitches that are crashing the system. To fix that malware, we have to look at the *Four CCs* that define our current reality.

Two of them are malware we need to *delete*. They are:

1. **Carbon Copy:** These are the mindless, habitual patterns that we replicate in order to appear "polite."

2. **Coercive Control:** This is a virus. It is the behavior that seeks to dominate, often without lifting a finger.

The other two are the new operating systems that we need to *save*.

1. **Consent Code:** This is the new, intentional programming that we must consciously choose to adopt to replace the software glitch.

2. **Community Care:** This is the widely circulated security system through which everyone runs the antivirus.

THE CARBON COPY (THE GLITCH)

We will not start with the bedroom. We will start with the text message.

A friend asks for a favor. The type of favor you genuinely enjoy saying yes to. You don't have the bandwidth. You're already stretched. Your gut says no. But then the code kicks in: *Don't be selfish. They'd do it for you. Just say yes.*

"Of course! Happy to help."

You resent them for a week. You resent yourself longer.

Why does this matter? Because every time we override our internal "no" in the small moments, we're rehearsing for the big ones. The script doesn't know the difference between a favor and a boundary. You're not broken. You were just running a Carbon Copy.

Acknowledging that we are just running a script, we can begin executing empowering scripts. The code instructed you, "Be polite. Don't make the situation awkward. Don't hurt their feelings." In other words, the code made you prioritize others' comfort over your own reality. *Why does this matter?* It matters because if you can so easily run the *Be Polite* script in such a low-stakes moment, it means you are ultimately better conditioned to run it in the high-stakes moment of a date, where your regret may be far greater due to the risk of not only a non-consensual physical violation of your body but also a dent in your overall self-esteem. We have only installed a backdoor for the virus. You were not broken; you were merely running a Carbon Copy.

COERCIVE CONTROL (THE VIRUS)

Bad code runs silently. Good code runs intentionally. Here, we understand the difference.

Now, let us examine the virus that exploits the backdoor: *Coercive Control.* For many more years than we care to remember, women have been gaslit into believing that if they didn't hold a knife to your throat, they were not engaging in "real" violence and that it was nothing more than a benign encounter; a "gray area," so to speak. Nothing could be further from the truth, and I am here to tell you that the Federal Government of the United States completely disagrees with that assertion. These are the facts as backed by statutory definition. *22 U.S.C. § 7102* provides the official legal definitions for terms used in the *Trafficking Victims Protection Act (TVPA),* a key U.S. law that seeks to combat human trafficking, and it defines "coercion" and other terms. Our focus in this book is "coercion." In the TVPA, coercion is defined as threats of serious harm, abuse of the legal process, or schemes intended to cause a person to believe they will be harmed if they don't comply.

Crucially, it is important to note that restraint is *not* required to arrive at a conclusion that "coercion" is involved. The law recognizes that you can be forced into a sexual act without even being touched. *Has your reputation been threatened? That is coercion. Have you been subjected to financial manipulation in any form? That is coercion. Have you been isolated to the point where you feel you have no exit? That is coercion.* To express matters with total clarity, if you felt forced, you were forced. It is as simple and as unambiguous as that. The law merely validates what your intuition has known all along. To grasp matters in proper context, coercive control is when someone repeatedly hurts, scares, or isolates another person to control them, and examples involve forcing or manipulating someone to act against their will, using threats; physical, emotional, financial, reputational, or control tactics like isolation, constant monitoring through texts and location, controlling finances and behavior, gaslighting, and threats to harm loved ones or pets. It is all about eroding independence and creating dependency through fear and pressure.

THE UNREPORTED CODE (THE SYSTEM CRASH)

We have examined the virus at the individual level. But here is what happens when you run that virus on a massive scale. The system crashes into silence. The data is undeniable. According to the Summer 2023 issue of the *Ballard Brief*, "Sexual assault is a highly prevalent yet rarely addressed issue within the United States. It is considered the most underreported and dismissed crime."

- 75% of sexual assaults go unreported

- On campuses, 95%

- 98% of perpetrators are never held accountable

- This isn't millions of people failing to speak

- This is a system coded to produce silence

Why is this so? It is so because the "Old Code" running in the background is designed to produce silence. Again, the *Ballard Brief* reports that there are various reasons why sexual assault cases are largely underreported or dismissed. There is a general misunderstanding of sexual assault, many rape myths, and ample victim blaming. Other contributing factors include knowledge of the identity of the perpetrator, power implications, an investigation process designed for the system instead of for humans, inefficiencies in the court process, and a lack of faith in the justice system. The underreporting and dismissal of sexual assault cases often lead to victims feeling guilt and worry about the perpetrator roaming free, and a greater risk of repeated crime.

The largest organization working to combat sexual assault and support survivors is the *Rape, Abuse, and Incest National Network (RAINN)*. RAINN reports that 20% of victims fear retaliation from the perpetrator or society, 13% of them believe the police wouldn't do anything to help, 8% didn't think it was important enough. So, what we have here is the classic "Old Code" script: *If assault happens, take refuge in shame and self-blame. After all, no one will believe me anyway. Stay Silent.* By no means can this be considered an individual failure. When nearly 98% of perpetrators are never held fully accountable, we are not looking at millions of people failing to speak up. Rather, what we are looking at is a system that was coded to produce silence.

THE CONSENT CODE (THE UPGRADE)

We've identified the glitch. Now we install the upgrade.

The Consent Code is not a contract signed in triplicate. The word comes from the Latin *consentire* — "to feel together." It's a shared understanding created through transparency and boundaries.

Here's the principle that changes everything: Consent becomes common when it's embedded, not explained.

Newton's First Law of Motion — the Law of Inertia — states that "an object in motion stays in motion with the same speed and in the same direction unless acted upon by an unbalanced external force." We don't teach people the physics of seatbelts. We built the seatbelt into the car. Click-clack. Ritual. Done.

The goal is to build "checking in" into human connection so deeply that it feels strange not to. But we need an operational framework to get there.

THE OPERATIONAL FRAMEWORK - DELETE. EDIT. SAVE

Let me give you a debugger.

DELETE — EDIT — SAVE

Run it on the "Unreported" script:

Old Code: If assault happens — shame — self-blame — silence.

The Upgrade: DELETE shame — that was never your code to carry. DELETE self-blame — the bug is in their system, not yours. INSTALL community care network.

Output: You get to decide what's next. Your timeline is yours.

Run it on a date:

Old Code: He pays for dinner — I owe him access — DELETE.

New Code: He pays for dinner — That was a gift — I express gratitude but maintain my boundary — SAVE.

We didn't stop the kindness. We deleted the transactional obligation. We're retraining the algorithm.

COMMUNITY CARE (THE ANTIVIRUS)

If Coercive Control is the virus, Community Care is the distributed security system. Simple concept: protect the whole network, not just one node. If one person is targeted, the others respond.

This is where men ask different questions — not "Hey man, step back and let this couple off the plane" but "Hey friend, how does she feel about this situation?" This is where women intervene when a friend starts fading at the bar. The predator can't find a host when the whole community is running the same antivirus.

We have moved from Coercive Control (Isolation) to Community Care (Connection).

HARDWARE FOR THE NEW CODE

I'm an operator. Operators like tools. Software updates need hardware to run on — and the best hardware is what people already use.

- **The "One Finger, Two Finger, Three" Signal:** Sometimes words fail. One finger = Red/Stop. Two fingers = Yellow/Pause. Three fingers = Green/Go. No speech required. Consent becomes visible. (Will be available as an app)

- **The Check-In Ritual:** Before the car moves, the seatbelt clicks. Before the moment escalates, a question lands. "Still good?" Two words. Build it into the sequence until skipping it feels as wrong as driving unbuckled.

- **The Group Text Protocol:** Friends going out? One person is the anchor. Check-ins happen. "You good?" isn't nagging — it's the network running its scan.

- **The Wearable Possibility:** Imagine biometric data validating your gut. Heart rate spiked? That's truth data. The tech exists. The integration is coming.

The point isn't any single tool. The point is embedding the Consent Code into rituals, signals, and systems people already trust — until checking in is as automatic as buckling up.

STATE OF THE UNION

Right now, your zip code determines your protection.

The Glitch: Over 75% of states still require proof of force for rape.

The Goal: State-level criminal codes reflecting a definition of and proactive awareness of consent.

The Proof: New Jersey has required "affirmative permission" since 1992 — a clear, conscious, voluntary "yes" that is ongoing and revocable. Result? Lowest rape rate in the nation: 17 per 100,000 — less than half the national average. Colorado installed the same update in 2022. Within two years: 26% drop, unanimous bipartisan support.

When we change the operating system from *"Did she resist?"* to *"Did she agree?"* — the violence drops. Good code scales.

CONCLUSION

I invite you to take your own action. You don't have to Carbon Copy your way through life. This is your framework for affirmative action and control:

- **Delete** the obligation

- **Edit** the script

- **Save** the boundary

Everything is to your advantage. The law is on your side. The data is on your side. The results are in. The update works.

This week, run the debugger once. One "no" you've been swallowing. One check-in you've been skipping. One boundary you've been copy-pasting around. Delete it. Edit it. Save yourself the crash.

CHAPTER FOUR

THE SHAME CODE

Deleting Victim Blaming

"I remember also what he was wearing that night even though it's true that no one has ever asked." — From the poem "What I Was Wearing" by Dr. Mary Simmerling

The Glitch In The Motherboard

The motherboard is the backbone of every computer — the central hub connecting all critical components so the system functions as a whole. Ours has malware. That malware expresses itself in a single, tragic sentence: "What were you wearing?"

We need to talk about the person who says it. Not the stranger on the internet — the one who matters. The mentor. The elder. The respected voice in your family, your community, your congregation. The person whose opinion carries weight because they've earned it through years of showing up. You know who they are in your life.

When something happens to you — or to someone you love — this person runs an automatic script: *That's terrible, honey. But what were you doing there so late?* Or the classic: *Well, that skirt was a little short, wasn't it?*

To a survivor, this can feel like a betrayal. I see it differently.

This isn't malice. It's malware.

That mentor is running Carbon Copy code — a survival script from a different era, copy-pasted into their consciousness by a society programmed to shift blame from predator to victim. In their mind, the logic runs: *If I can find the reason you messed up, I can convince myself that if I avoid that mistake, I'll be safe.*

This script has a name. Psychologists call it the *Just World Hypothesis* — a cognitive bias where people believe the world is inherently fair, that good people are rewarded and bad people are punished. It provides a false sense of order. But it also causes people to blame victims: *They must have done something to deserve it.* It ignores context. It rationalizes injustice. It kills empathy.

The connection to Maslow is clear — safety sits at the foundation of human needs. Your mentor's script is a desperate attempt to keep that foundation intact. But here's the tragedy: the very notion of safety is already at risk, especially for those with vulnerable signatures. The code doesn't protect anyone. It just redistributes the shame.

INTENDED AS LOVE. WRAPPED IN FEAR. DELIVERED AS SHAME

Intentions don't justify consequences. When the consequence is system failure, the intention is irrelevant. This code has failed our social system and is crashing our justice system.

THE BOTTLENECK: 975 LOST CASES

In business, a sales funnel visualizes the journey from first contact to closed deal. You start wide — everyone who sees your product — and narrow down through stages: awareness, interest, decision, purchase. At each stage, some people drop off. That's expected. The funnel helps you see where the friction is and what's actually converting.

Apply that lens to justice. The justice funnel tracks what happens between a crime occurring and a perpetrator being held accountable. At each stage — reporting, arrest, prosecution, conviction, incarceration — cases exit the system. Some exits are legitimate: insufficient evidence, false accusations, prosecutorial discretion, innocence. The system is designed with safeguards. That's not failure — that's due process.

But when 97.5% of cases exit before accountability, we're not looking at due process. We're looking at systemic friction. The question isn't whether the funnel should narrow — it should. The question is *why* it narrows so drastically for this category of crime, and *where* the friction actually resides.

The data tells the story. According to *Rape, Abuse & Incest National Network (RAINN)*, corroborated by the DOJ and FBI: of every 1,000 sexual assaults that occur, only 310 are reported. Only 50 lead to an arrest. Only 28 lead to felony convictions. Only 25 result in incarceration.

98% of perpetrators walk free.

That's a 98% exit rate between occurrence and accountability. Some of those exits are due to the system working — protecting the innocent, requiring proof, exercising discretion. But the sheer scale indicates that something else is happening. When Detroit tested its backlogged rape kits, 35% of identified perpetrators were serial offenders. These weren't cases that exited because of innocence. They exited because the system didn't pursue them.

Here's a business perspective: If I ran a logistics company and lost 975 out of every 1,000 packages, I wouldn't be in business. I'd be under investigation for negligence. My customers would leave. My reputation would be gone. And I certainly wouldn't be elected to top roles in the federal government.

The justice funnel isn't broken because it narrows. It's broken because of *where* it narrows — and *why*.

Victim blaming is the primary friction point creating this loss. This is what victim blaming does. It stops the report because of the *They won't believe me* narrative. It stops the arrest because of the *She was drinking. It is a messy situation* narrative. It stops the prosecution because of the *She's not a 'perfect victim* narrative. We are running a system that requires a victim to be sober, chaste, and physically bruised to be believed. We are asking the victim to be perfect while we ask the predator to simply be present. Worse, we often allow him to be present more than once. That is the tragicomedy of the victim code.

The Perfect Victim checklist runs like malware: Was she sober? Did she fight back? Is her sexual history "clean"? Did she report immediately? Is there physical evidence of resistance? Most assaults don't fit this script. The system was designed to require it anyway.

But why is the silence so loud? The silence is deafening for *carbon copy* reasons. Victim blaming creates specific psychological barriers that contribute to this silence. The system was designed to foster silence, so these are not individual failures on the part of victims. The *Brennan Center for Justice*, an organization that tracks Department of Justice (DOJ) reports, states that 20% of victims worry about retaliation, not just from the perpetrator but also from society. Thirteen percent believe the police will not take action, while 8% feel it is "not important enough" to report. Yet, there is a deeper psychology at play. *PubMed*, a City University of New York (CUNY) research platform, found that for adult women, the primary reason for not reporting is a combination of *guilt and embarrassment.* There is also the issue of the perpetrator's relationship. The most commonly identified barrier is the relationship the survivor has with the perpetrator. Survivors are often met at the agency level with skepticism about the motivations behind their decisions to report. In the final analysis, when 63-80% of sexual assaults go unreported, we are not witnessing millions of individual *failures to report.* Rather, we are observing a system that is *coded* to produce silence.

HIGH INTELLIGENCE QUOTIENT (IQ); LOW CONSENT QUOTIENT (CQ)

You will be forgiven if you think that victim blaming occurs primarily as a consequence of ignorance and that it results from a lack of, or insufficient, education, possibly coupled with a deficit in overall sophistication. In other words, if people were smarter, they wouldn't blame the victim. You would be absolutely wrong. You might be shocked to discover that some of the most misguided minds on this subject are also among the brightest in the United States. Yes, even the "brightest minds" in the land hold this misguided belief. I will relate a recent story in this regard. Let me introduce you to Richard Stallman, a computer scientist at the Massachusetts Institute of Technology (MIT) and a genius in his field. He is considered an exceptionally brilliant man, having received several honorary doctorate degrees and the MacArthur "Genius Grant" in 1990. MIT, where he was a research scientist at the university's Computer Science and Artificial Intelligence Laboratory (CSAIL), regarded him as a rare type of intellectual asset. Sometime in 2019, Stallman, in a series of emails from a CSAIL group email list, stated that a 17-year-old girl who was allegedly instructed by

Epstein to have sex with one of his influential friends likely seemed *entirely willing* to engage in the act. Stallman also argued that it is unfair to label such an incident as *sexual assault.* To quote Stallman, "We can imagine many scenarios, but the most plausible scenario is that she presented herself to him as entirely willing." When someone on the email chain noted that the girl was 17 at the time, and that sex with a minor is statutory rape, Stallman replied, "I think it is morally absurd to define 'rape' in a way that depends on minor details such as which country it was in or whether the victim was 18 years old or 17."

Stallman's remarks drew criticism from computer scientists within and outside the MIT community, prompting some to dig through Stallman's past blog posts. This effort unearthed other writings in which Stallman expressed views on age and sexuality, including lowering acceptable age expectations for sensuality without citing supporting biology. In fact, according to NPR, the global news outlet, in its September 17, 2019 edition, *The Daily Beast* first reported that Stallman wrote in 2003, "I think that everyone age 14 or above ought to take part in sex, though not indiscriminately. Some people are ready earlier." In 2006, he wrote, "I am skeptical of the claim that voluntary pedophilia harms children. The arguments that it causes harm seem to be based on cases which aren't voluntary, which are then stretched by parents who are horrified by the idea that their little baby is maturing." More to the point regarding the dubious application of his intellect to an issue that is the source of trauma for many, Stallman attempted to debate the definition of sexual assault as if it were a line of code to be debugged, arguing over the "minor details" of age and jurisdiction. This is what happens when you have a high Intelligence Quotient (IQ) but a low Consent Quotient (CQ). Intellect, by its very nature, is fundamentally flawed by its total dependence on logic to rationalize even emotive situations. That is why intellect can weaponize victim blaming. It uses logic to rationalize the abuse. This is the process:

- **Rationalization:** It ingeniously constructs a scenario in which the predator is innocent.

- **Semantic Distraction:** It disingenuously argues over definitions rather than human reality.

- **Power Erasure:** It, both ingeniously and disingenuously, chooses to ignore the very obvious truths surrounding power constructs.

In the final analysis, intelligence does not inoculate you against bad code. In fact, it often helps you write more sophisticated excuses for that bad code.

FAILURE OF THE PROTECTION CODE: THE RAPE KIT CONUNDRUM

A warehouse has a simple, yet singular purpose. It is used for storing goods. *But, who would ever believe that victim blaming can be stored in a warehouse?* Incredibly, one of the most infamous stories of warehousing serves as the physical manifestation of victim blaming, and it is in the form of a massive backlog of rape kits. *What is the Rape Kit?* Let me tell you the story. As brilliantly outlined in Pagan Kennedy's *The Secret History of the Rape Kit - A True Crime Story*, it is the classic tale of *Protection Code failure*. As Pagan Kennedy relates in her book, in 1978, a woman named Martha Goddard invented the rape kit.

It was a brilliant tool designed to catch serial predators and help sexual assault survivors. The book itself is a historical detective story that blends true crime, biography, and social history to explore the origins of forensic evidence collection and the fight for women's recognition in science and law. Martha Goddard's story began in 1972 when she volunteered at a crisis hotline, counseling girls who had been molested by their fathers, teachers, and uncles. Soon, Martha found herself on a mission to answer a question: *Why were so many sexual predators getting away with their crimes?*

By the end of the decade, she had launched a campaign urging hospitals and police departments to collect evidence of sexual assault and treat survivors with dignity. Then, in 1978, she designed a new kind of forensic tool, the *Rape Kit*, along with new practices around evidence collection that spread across the country.

It started with a $10,000 grant from Playboy. Yes, the *Playboy Foundation* provided the initial and crucial funding for the development and distribution of the first standardized rape kit. Chicago-based Martha Goddard had found it extremely difficult to secure funding from conventional sources because *polite society* shied away from discussing the topic of rape. Through a connection, she finally acquired the necessary seed money and initial kits that were distributed to hospitals across Illinois as a pilot program. I will delve into the paradox of *vice* supporting *virtue* in a later chapter.

This is where the story becomes inexplicably complex. Today, the federal government has spent over $1.3 billion trying to fix the backlog of untested kits. *Why is there a backlog?* There is a backlog, not because the science doesn't work. There is a backlog because, for decades, police departments collected the evidence and simply decided not to test it. They "screened out" the cases. In the typical scenario, the detective decides that the victim isn't credible; she is a sex worker; she was high; she knew the guy. In other words, the system decided that her "value" wasn't worth the $1,000 cost of the test. *In Detroit, when they finally cleared a warehouse of 11,000 untested kits, some of which had been sitting there for decades, do you know what they found?* They discovered a staggering 841 serial offenders! These men didn't just rape

once. They raped again, and again, and again, because the system blamed the first victim and let the predator go. The baffling truth is that the backlog is not a funding problem; rather, it is a priority problem. More tragically, it is the physical manifestation of a society that would rather blame a woman for being drunk than apprehend a man who poses an extreme danger to society.

THE COUNTER-CODE

In 2013, Jen Brockman and Dr. Mary Wyandt-Hiebert created a visual debugger. The *What Were You Wearing?* exhibit displays recreated outfits survivors wore during their assaults, paired with their stories. Initiated at the University of Arkansas, it is now traveling globally.

You walk in expecting mini-skirts and stilettos. What you see: oversized sweatpants, a military uniform, a child's sundress, flannel pajamas, and a fast-food work uniform.

It stops you cold. The code that clothing equals consent — deleted on sight.

But here's the question we never ask: *What was the predator wearing?* As poet Mary Simmerling wrote, "I remember also what he was wearing that night, even though it's true that no one has ever asked." Suit, jersey, hoodie — we don't ask because we know his clothing didn't cause his behavior. He did.

The road has changed, but the code hasn't. Today the question isn't *Why did you walk down that road?* — it's *Why did you send that photo? Why did you give him your number? Why did you use that app?*

Same script. New platform. Consent given in one context doesn't transfer to another. A photo shared privately isn't permission to distribute. A number exchanged isn't an invitation for harassment.

The digital blame code runs the same malware:

Delete: "Why did you send that photo?" — *Replace:* "Why did he share it without consent?"

Until we update the code, predators exploit the gap between what's technically possible and what's actually permitted.

DELETE. EDIT. SAVE

The time has come for us to run a new sequence. It is not an optional need; it is a compelling need. We need to stop looking at individual failures and start fixing the operating system. This is the sequence. *Delete. Edit. Save.*

- **Delete the Shame Code.** The *Perfect Victim* is a myth. The idea that you can "safety proof" yourself by appearing chaste or modest is totally misguided. It is a lie. Delete the guilt. Delete the notion that it was your job to prevent a crime committed against you.

- **Edit the Question.** Stop asking, *Why did you go there?* Start asking, *Who did this?* Stop asking, *Why did you drink so much?* Start asking, *Why did he think your state of incapacitation was an opportunity for him to take advantage of you?*

- **Save the Community Care.** The antidote to victim blaming is *curiosity*. When someone finally finds the courage to share their traumatic experience, resist the urge to immediately adopt a judgmental stance. Instead, awaken the natural curiosity you possess as a human being. Find the words to say, *I am so sorry that happened. What do you need right now? How can I support you?* That is the *Community Care (CC)*code. It shifts the burden off the individual and places it back where it belongs: on the community to provide support and on the system to hold the predator accountable.

We no longer need to be *kind of human* about this. What we need now is *human kindness.* We must eliminate the operational bottleneck that is obstructing the natural course of justice. When we close the 975-case gap between *occurrence* and *incarceration,* we also stop blaming the 975, and then we might finally apprehend the predators who have truly violated the human code. We should reject any illusion about victim blaming. Victim blaming isn't just a social faux pas; it is an operational bottleneck that is costing us billions in taxpayer dollars.

CHAPTER FIVE

THE TOURIST

A Code for Desire

"Power over others is weakness disguised as strength."
Eckhart Tolle

We just spent a chapter deleting victim blaming. Before we explore the predator's operating system, we need to discuss something else first: desire.

Not predatory desire. Not coercive desire. Just... desire.

The pleasure industry has existed for centuries. It's a multi-billion dollar ecosystem that society simultaneously consumes and condemns. We buy the products, watch the content, visit the clubs — then shake our heads at the people who make it all possible. This hypocrisy isn't the point of this chapter. The point is that buried inside this ecosystem is a distinction most people never learn to make.

The distinction between the *Playboy* and the *Predator*.

THE KEY DISTINCTION

A "playboy" — in the cultural sense — refers to someone who lives on their own terms, enjoys company, and is unapologetically oriented toward pleasure. The word carries baggage. It implies wealth, carelessness, and maybe even recklessness. But strip away the judgment and look at the underlying code.

A true Playboy needs *enthusiasm* to get off.

A Predator needs *control* to get off.

This is the key distinction. Write it down. Teach it to your kids. It changes everything.

The Playboy archetype — whatever term you prefer — genuinely enjoys company. They're transparent about their desires. Their satisfaction depends entirely on the other person being just as into the encounter as they are. Mutual enthusiasm isn't a bonus; it's a requirement. Without it, there's no charge. No spark. No point. Playmate, Playgirl, Playboy, Play is the vibe.

The Predator operates on the opposite fuel. They seek vulnerability, not enthusiasm. They rely on silence, blurred lines, and power imbalances. Their tactics involve grooming: excessive flattery, gift-giving, creating secrecy ("just between us"), isolating victims from support systems, pushing boundaries incrementally, and manufacturing guilt or obligation. The goal is *control* — and they derive pleasure from having it.

Here's the tragedy of the old code: society often confuses these two. When we tell young men that simply *wanting* sex makes them predatory, we corrupt their programming. Desire is healthy. Pursuit is healthy. The distinction is that healthy pursuit requires a co-pilot who's enjoying the ride just as much as you are.

Women find pursuit *hot* — when it's mutual. When the energy matches. When both people are leaning in. That mutuality is the entire game.

Predators can be diffused by empowered systems — clear boundaries, accountability structures, and communities that believe victims. Playboys don't need to be diffused. They need partners who match their energy.

THE PROBLEM WITH THE OLD CODE

Society has one recommended relationship model: *The Resident.*

Long-term. Committed. Build-a-life-together. For many people, this is the goal — and it's a beautiful one. The safety of deep knowledge, the fortress of a committed partner, the compounding returns of decades together. Nothing in this chapter diminishes that.

But the old code made a critical error. It declared this the *only* valid operating system.

It's not.

Some people — or certain people at certain stages of life — are *Tourists*.

A Tourist visits. They bring great energy. They appreciate and enjoy the destination. They have a wonderful time, contribute to the experience, and then go home. There's nothing wrong with being a Tourist.

The problem isn't tourism. The problem is *lying about your itinerary*.

The old code created shame around non-Resident lifestyles. That shame produced deception. People who wanted to be Tourists pretended to be Residents just to get through the door. They faked long-term intentions to access short-term experiences. This is where harm enters — not from the desire itself, but from the dishonesty that shame produced.

If a person feels free to say, "I'm just visiting right now, but I'd love to take you to dinner," that's honest. That's the Consent Code in operation. It allows the other person to decide: *Am I open to visitors?*

Some people are. Some aren't. Both answers are valid.

To change the code, we start by eliminating the shame from these different modes. When we validate the Tourist, they don't need to lie. When we stop treating non-Resident desire as broken, people can be honest about what they're actually offering.

Honesty is the upgrade. Not the lifestyle itself — the *honesty* about the lifestyle.

THE SHAME GAME

The "Playboy" label signals agency: *I chose this.*

The historical female equivalents — slut, loose, easy, broken — signal passivity: *This happened to me.*

See the asymmetry? A man who pursues pleasure is living a lifestyle. A woman who pursues pleasure has something wrong with her. The old code pathologized female desire while celebrating male desire. Both were running the same operating system — enthusiasm for connection — but only one faced shame for it.

If a woman is transparent about seeking pleasure, variety, or casual connection, the old code labels her a "femme fatale" — French for "fatal woman." She's seen as dangerous, manipulative, and morally ambiguous. In reality, she might just be someone who knows what she wants and isn't pretending otherwise when it doesn't fit someone else's narrative.

The shame serves no one. It doesn't protect anyone. It just drives behavior underground, where honesty dies and harm multiplies.

THE SAMANTHA JONES TEST

Consider Samantha Jones from *Sex and the City*. High volume. Zero shame. Obsessed with *her* pleasure. Clear on her boundaries — never crosses others'. Every partner is enthusiastic; none are coerced.

The old code called her broken, desperate, and unable to commit. The new code sees something different: a Sovereign who knows exactly what she wants and doesn't pretend otherwise. Her honesty is her protection code — for herself and her partners.

Notice what's absent from her storylines: manipulation, coercion, and deception about intentions. She doesn't pretend to want Residency to access a one-night visit. She doesn't guilt partners into staying. She doesn't need *control* — she needs *enthusiasm*. When she doesn't get it, she moves on.

You don't have to be Samantha. But you can learn from her clarity.

The test is simple: Could your behavior fit into a Samantha Jones plotline without the audience recoiling? If yes, you're running clean code. If the writers would have to frame you as the villain, examine why.

UPGRADING THE TERMINOLOGY

To rewrite the code, we can start by upgrading the language. We need terms that honor choice and agency rather than implying passivity or shame.

The Libertine: The historical counterpart to *prude*. A libertine has a philosophy of pleasure—intentional, considered, unapologetic. The code: *I'm not loose; I'm a libertine. I have a philosophy of pleasure.*

The Bon Vivant: French for *one who lives well*. Sex is one course in a banquet that includes good food, travel, art, and company. The Bon Vivant doesn't hunt for connection; they savor life. Intimacy is part of a rich existence, not the sole focus.

The Sovereign: A sovereign entity answers to no one. They choose who enters their borders, for how long, and under what terms. The code: *I don't belong to you. I am a sovereign state.*

Solo Poly: Someone who maintains multiple intimate connections but identifies as their own primary partner. They're not seeking the "relationship escalator"—cohabitation, marriage, merger. The code: *I am complete on my own, but I welcome visitors.*

The Free Agent: A sports metaphor. High-value, highly skilled, currently unsigned. They can play for any team they choose, for as long as the contract serves them. There's no shame in being unsigned—it's a position of strength.

The Pleasure Activist: Coined by Adrienne Maree brown. Seeking pleasure as an act of resistance against systems that want you miserable and compliant. The code: *My joy is my resistance.*

THE TOURIST FRAMEWORK

Let's make it operational.

The Resident commits to a destination. They buy property, learn the neighborhood, and invest in the long-term infrastructure of a shared life. This is beautiful, and most of society's support systems are built around it.

The Tourist visits. They bring energy, appreciation, and presence. They contribute to the experience. They don't pretend the trip is permanent, and they don't trash the place on the way out. They clean up after themselves and leave the destination better than they found it.

Both are valid. The friction comes from misrepresentation.

A Tourist pretending to be a Resident—to gain access, to avoid judgment, to skip the honest conversation—causes harm. Not because tourism is wrong, but because deception is wrong.

A Resident who secretly wishes they were a Tourist—trapped by expectation, resentful of commitment, going through the motions—also causes harm. Different harm, same root: the inability to be honest about what you actually want.

The Consent Code asks one question: *What are you actually offering?*

Answer honestly. Let the other person decide if they're interested in that offer. If yes, proceed with mutual enthusiasm. If no, respect the boundary and move on.

This isn't complicated. The old code made it complicated by loading desire with shame, which made honesty feel dangerous and produced the very deceptions that cause real harm.

A NOTE ON PURSUIT

One of the most damaging messages the old code sends to young men is: *Your desire is inherently predatory.*

This is false. And it's dangerous.

Desire is not predation. Pursuit is not assault. Wanting connection — physical, emotional, romantic — is not a character flaw. It's human.

The distinction is *mutuality*.

Pursuit becomes problematic when it ignores signals, continues past "no," uses pressure, guilt, or position to manufacture compliance, or treats another person as an objective to be achieved rather than a human with their own desires and boundaries.

But pursuit that reads the room? Does that calibrate to the response? Does that person get genuinely excited when the other person is excited too? That's not predation. That's the connection.

We need to teach this distinction clearly. When we tell young men that *all* sexual desire is suspect, we don't reduce harm — we just confuse the honest ones while the actual predators ignore the message entirely.

The goal isn't to eliminate desire. The goal is to channel it toward mutual enthusiasm. That's the Consent Code.

THE OPERATIONAL TAKEAWAY

This chapter isn't a permission slip to act like a Playboy. It's a framework for understanding desire — yours and others.

Ask yourself: *Do I need enthusiasm to feel satisfied, or do I need control?*

If your satisfaction depends on mutual excitement — if the other person's genuine interest is what makes it good — you're running clean code. If your satisfaction depends on having power over someone, on compliance rather than enthusiasm, on blurred lines and plausible deniability — that's predator code. Get help.

Validate the Tourists so they don't need to lie.

Respect the Residents without treating them as the only valid option.

Teach the next generation that wanting connection is good — as long as the enthusiasm is mutual.

Whether you're a Resident or a Tourist, the visit should be worthwhile for everyone involved.

YOUR ASSIGNMENTS

The DELETE Command

Write down a word you've been called — or called yourself — that carries shame. *Slut. Player. Easy. Broken. Commitment-phobe. Whore. Man-whore. Loose.*

Now select a replacement from the menu: *Libertine. Sovereign. Bon Vivant. Tourist. Free Agent. Pleasure Activist.*

Write both words. Cross out the old one.

That's a DELETE command. You just rewrote a line of your own code.

THE HONEST ITINERARY

Before your next encounter — casual or otherwise — answer three questions out loud or on paper:

- *What am I actually offering?* (Residency? A visit? One night? Ongoing but undefined?)

- *What do I actually want from this?* (Connection? Release? Companionship? Exploration?)

- *Am I willing to say this honestly to the other person?*

If you can't answer #3 with yes, you're not ready for the encounter. The Consent Code requires honesty — with yourself first, then with them.

CHAPTER SIX

THE TRAGIC MYSTIQUE OF PORN

Humans iterate. So does porn.

"Stop choking people without first talking or asking about it. Just stop."
Dr. Debby Herbenick, Indiana University, lead investigator of the National Survey of Sexual Health and Behavior

Cave walls. Print. Film. Screens. Internet. Each technological leap has made sexual content more accessible, more private, more extreme. What once required seeking out now finds you. What once shocked now bores. The pattern isn't new — but the scale is.

Here's what changed: porn is no longer a thing you watch. For a generation raised on high-speed internet, it's become source code — the default script for how sex is supposed to look, sound, and feel. The problem isn't that people watch porn. The problem arises when that code gets Carbon Copied into real encounters without a single line of conversation.

Violence depicted on screen is being replicated in bedrooms without discussion or consent. A whole generation learned the choreography but skipped the negotiation that precedes professional performance.

And there's a hardware problem too: when your brain gets trained on supranormal stimuli — images engineered for maximum dopamine — real partner sex may no longer trigger sufficient arousal. You become wired for the pixel, not the person.

Challenge One: Porn has become the source code — the default script people run during real encounters without questioning whether their partner signed up for that scene.

Challenge Two: Porn is often the *first* source — the entry point. For 73% of teens, mainstream porn is their sex education. Median first exposure: age 12. When your first lesson in intimacy involves choking, gagging, and zero negotiation, that's the baseline you carry into your first real encounter.

Two glitches. Same root: a generation learned the choreography before they learned the conversation.

THE NEW EPIDEMIC

Half of people who've been choked during sex say it wasn't always consensual. Not a niche kink gone wrong — half.

And here's the operational absurdity of "safe choking": You're in the middle of sex. Aroused. Distracted. Now you're supposed to know your partner's neck anatomy well enough to avoid the carotid arteries, track 8-10 seconds precisely before unconsciousness hits, apply less than 5 lbs of pressure (less than it takes to open a soda can), and somehow maintain that awareness while your brain is flooded with dopamine. You don't squeeze until you see blue — the window is seconds, and damage can be invisible, delayed by days or weeks.

This isn't a skill most people have. This is a responsibility for protection that most people aren't trained for.

As Brian Bennett, a law enforcement veteran, put it: *There is no safe way to strangle another person.*

The UK agreed. In 2025, they banned choking in pornography. Andrea Simon of the End Violence Against Women Coalition explained: *Women can't consent to the long-term harm caused by it, such as impaired cognitive functioning and memory. There is no such thing as safe strangulation.*

The script got copied. The consent negotiation got skipped. And the physical reality — 5 lbs, 8 seconds — doesn't care whether you meant well.

THE AGENCY SHIFT

Who owns the code? For decades, studios owned the women. The "Reference Man" called the shots.

The Creator Economy changed that. OnlyFans generated

$6.6 billion in 2023 — 300 million accounts, 70% male consumers, 4.1 million creators, 84% women. The structure flipped. Women moved from being inventory to becoming owners. When a woman owns the channel, she owns the consent. That's a shift from exploitation code to agency code. The creator economy removes the middleman and puts boundary-setting power back in the performer's hands.

There's also the concept of ethical porn — adult content produced with a focus on safety, consent, fair pay, and performer agency. Unlike mainstream porn, ethical porn centers on mutual pleasure, often depicts aftercare and communication, and features diverse bodies and realistic encounters. The catch: *You cannot be an ethical consumer of porn if you aren't paying for your porn.* Free tube sites run on stolen content, lack performer compensation, and may contain trafficking material. If the product is free, someone else is paying — often the person on screen.

Regardless of your moral stance on the content, the consent architecture matters.

THE FIRE PROBLEM

Scott Galloway calls pornography "the McDonald's of sex — fast, convenient, and utterly divorced from nutrition."

In a study of 2,000 American adults, 11% of men reported agreeing with the statement "I am addicted to pornography." Dr. Anna Lembke, a Stanford psychiatrist and author of *Dopamine Nation*, has tracked warning signs since the early

2000s in male patients who self-describe as porn addicts.

Here's the cost Galloway identifies: *Porn can reduce your ambition to take risks, become a better person, and build a better life.* The skills developed in the pursuit of organic connection — resilience, reading social cues, expressing interest while making someone feel safe — atrophy when a screen becomes the path of least resistance.

His data point: 51% of men aged 18-24 have never asked a woman out in person.

The fire that fuels mating is the same fire that fuels ambition. Dampen one, and you dampen both.

FIXING THE GLITCH

Watch the performance if you want to enjoy it. But don't bring that script into your bedroom without asking your co-star if they want to play that role.

DELETE the assumption that porn is a tutorial.

EDIT your understanding of aggression. Violence is not a default setting — it's a negotiated edge case.

SAVE the conversation. If you can't talk about it, you aren't ready to engage in it.

CHAPTER SEVEN

THE COERCIVE PREDATOR

"No more than anybody else that I've been with."
Brock Turner, sexual assault convict

I will waste no time introducing the predator because to tackle him, you must know who he *really* is.

The predator exploits through a sustained pattern of manipulation and coercion. His playbook is repetitive — grooming tactics to build trust and dependency before violating boundaries. He is always accompanied by a need for *dominance* and *control*, disregarding personal boundaries while treating consent as interference.

But make no mistake: predators are not monsters. They are *operators* who have developed uncommon efficiency running a specific source code. The solution is not to fix them — it's to build enough friction into the system that their code becomes obsolete.

THE BASELINE ERROR

Two Swedish graduate students cycling across Stanford's campus at 1 a.m. found Brock Turner on top of an unconscious woman behind a dumpster. They confronted him. He ran. They tackled him. There was a moment of testimony that revealed the entire error in our operating system. Malcolm Gladwell, in his 2019 book, *Talking to Strangers: What We Should Know about the People We Don't Know*, highlighted this error in our operating system, and it stops you cold. At trial, the prosecutor played a voicemail from that night — the victim's voice slurred and incoherent.

You would agree with me that in that voicemail she sounded super intoxicated, right?

Turner's response: *No more than anybody else that I've been with.*

That line reveals everything. He wasn't describing an anomaly; he was describing his baseline. A woman in a state of incapacitation wasn't a stop sign — it was just the environment he operated in.

Is it normal for you to pick up a drunk girl? the prosecutor asked.

At a party, yes.

This is the predator's operating system exposed in real-time: scanning for vulnerability, normalizing exploitation, and lacking consent intelligence.

THE ALGORITHM IS NOT MAGIC, IT IS PHYSICS

An algorithm is a step-by-step set of instructions or rules designed to solve a specific problem or perform a computation, with each instruction being clear, sequential, and unambiguous, leaving no room for erroneous interpretation. Ultimately, it takes data as input and transforms it into useful information as output. A common example is the baking of a cake. The recipe is the algorithm, the ingredients are the input, and the cake itself is the output. Predators employ the principle of the algorithm in their mission. They *input* data they are already familiar with to get their *output*. Predators do not choose their victims at random; they run a *Vulnerability Scan* as their algorithm.

In a landmark 1981 study, researchers filmed people walking down a New York City street and showed the tapes to inmates convicted of violent assaults. The study, by Grayson and Stein, was incredibly simple. It involved setting up a video camera on a street in New York City, filming 60 people as they walked by between 10:00 AM and 12:00 PM over a three-day period, and then showing the footage to 12 convicted violent offenders, asking them to select those individuals they would target on a scale of 1 to 10, in order to discover if there were any identifiable non-verbal cues that were commonly recognized. A second set of 53 inmates reviewed the tapes to confirm or establish the rating scale. The offenders didn't know the people on the screen. They couldn't hear them; they just watched them walk. The result was striking: offenders showed 90% agreement on who was a vulnerable target. It wasn't about size. It wasn't about gender. It was about *gait* kinematics: stride length, fluidity, or weight shift. Offenders with high psychopathy scores could read these biomechanical cues the way a stock market day trader reads a ticker tape at the New York Stock Exchange. This isn't magic. It is a sharable scanning code used to identify targets who seem ungrounded, unaware, or unsupported — and it fails against those who are embodied, alert, and connected.

Predators don't choose randomly. They select based on *ease of access* — and the scan is specific. They're reading embodiment cues: nervous system signatures that suggest prior victimization, unprocessed trauma, or a pattern of overriding one's own boundaries. Posture, gait, pace — the body broadcasts what the mind has experienced.

This is why they test with small boundary pushes first: a too-close stand, an unreasonable ask. They're not just testing compliance — they're calibrating. A target who pushes back is hard. A target who accommodates is soft.

Women know this code exists, even without a name for it. That's why they run expensive *masking protocols* — keys in hand, fake phone calls, projecting a confidence they may not feel. This is the *Safety Tax*: the energy spent jamming the signal before they even leave the house.

The algorithm was built for a different era. The environment is changing in ways predators don't yet understand.

THE ECOSYSTEM IS BIGGER THAN ONE GUY

We think of the predator as a *Lone Wolf.* It's an absolute myth. Every major predator requires a *lattice of enablers* — legal, institutional, and digital — to operate at scale.

THE DEMAND SIDE: NTH ROOM

In South Korea, a network of Telegram chatrooms trafficked coerced sexual content of women and minors from 2018 to 2020. The two operators were eventually imprisoned. But here's a number that should stop you: 260,000 users paid $200 to $1,200 each, totaling $130 million in revenue. There is no stadium in America that holds 260,000 people. This wasn't a room — it was a city. The *predator* was simply the CEO. The users were the shareholders.

THE INSTITUTIONAL COVER: LARRY NASSAR

332 survivors. A $500 million settlement. A team doctor who operated for 22 years — often with parents in the room. Nassar didn't hide in alleys; he hacked the *medical trust* code, disguising assault as *pelvic floor therapy.* When it surfaced, MSU's initial response was tepid: "Good luck; I am on your side." Rachael Denhollander proved that a young girl couldn't trust *any* adults in the network — coaches, doctors, or university leaders. There was gross negligence regarding the entire protection code.

THE SILENCE CODE: JEFFREY EPSTEIN

Federal investigators estimated over 1,000 victims. Only 150 received compensation. The 85% gap proves how well the Silence Code works.

THE ECOSYSTEM MATH

Case	Victims/Users	Duration	Enabler Type
Nth Room	260,000 paying users	2 years	Digital demand
Nassar	332 survivors	22 years	Institutional cover
Epstein	1,000+ estimated	20+ years	Systemic impunity

The predator's greatest asset is darkness. Not literal darkness — operational invisibility. He relies on silence, on isolation, and on the assumption that each victim believes she is alone. This is why mega-cases take decades to surface. This is why the Silence Code is so effective. Every predator runs the same calculation: *If I stay invisible, I stay operational.*

The math we're about to look at proves how well that calculation has worked — and why breaking the silence breaks the code.

THE MATH OF THE "ONE-AND-DONE" MYTH

There's a cultural myth that sexual violence is widespread because *men are animals.* False. The vast majority of men are protectors, partners, and allies who value consensual sex. The truth is that sexual violence is industrialized by a small group of career offenders.

The 6% Reality Check: Lisak & Miller found that approximately 6% of men were responsible for assaults.

The Volume Check: Within that 6%, 63% were repeat offenders — averaging 5.8 rapes each.

Multiple subsequent studies have replicated the serial offender finding. *The bad apples* theory is mathematically valid. A small percentage of malware is corrupting the entire network.

The culture compounds it. We blame victims through rape myths and normalize sexualized violence. We replicate the overlooking of assault coupled with low accountability. The malware stays operational.

Case in point: Michael Love. In 2019, this Mississippi resident received six life sentences for kidnapping and sexually assaulting six Memphis women between 2008 and 2015. He used false identities on social media to meet targets, held them against their will, and then abandoned them in deserted areas. Each woman reported the incidents. DNA was collected and preserved in sexual assault kits for each case. When Love was finally arrested in 2015 and his DNA was entered into the system, it linked him to all six cases.

Six life sentences. Because the kits were finally tested. That's what happens when the system stops losing evidence.

THE LOST SEX ECONOMY

One thing we need to quickly do is exculpate another frequently accused entity: *male sexual desire*. Male sexual desire is not the enemy, and neither is high libido, the desire to conquer, the thrill of the chase, or the craving for connection. These are healthy, vital parts of the human experience. We want more sex. We want more pleasure. We want men to feel safe while expressing their drive. We want women to feel safe to explore it.

The romantic recession has multiple causes — but the predator's specific toll is converting enthusiasm into vigilance.

Every unit of energy a woman spends scanning for threats, watching her drink, or tracking her exit points is a unit she cannot spend on connection, play, or pleasure. When safety protocols run this high, libido itself is throttled. She's on guard — not because she's frigid, but because she doesn't want to end up in a morgue.

The Safety Tax women pay creates a massive opportunity cost for men too. By eliminating the predator's code, we aren't just preventing harm — we're unlocking enthusiasm currently trapped behind a firewall of fear.

The Fear Metric is real: 1 in 3 single women believe "most men" would take sexual advantage of them if given the opportunity. 54% feel pessimistic about dating due to the labor of vetting for safety. They're running *Security Protocols* instead of *Connection Protocols*.

Gentlemen: the safer she feels, the wilder she can be.

THE PIVOT FROM SILENCE TO FRICTION

For decades, the system has relied on *Silence*. The predator counts on our politeness — that we won't cause a scene, that we'll treat each incident as isolated. We've been operating under the *Docile Code*.

We're shifting to *Friction*.

We don't need to fight them. We don't need to scream. We just need to update the environment so their code stops executing. Think of it like updating your phone's operating system — the old buggy apps just crash. They don't launch. That's what we're doing to predatory behavior.

WHAT CREATES FRICTION?

Connection. Presence. Awareness. Not vigilance — just humans acting like humans who see each other.

When you're out with friends and something feels off about an interaction — not yours, but someone else's — that signal is data. You don't need to diagnose it. You don't need to accuse anyone. You just don't have to leave.

Staying isn't about freezing in place when your own spine jumps. It's about not abandoning the people you came with. Not peeling off because someone new arrived and you don't want to "third wheel." Real connection welcomes company. Coercion requires isolation. If your presence is a problem, that tells you something.

Using names matters too — not as a tactic, but as a practice. We've become an anonymous culture. Eyes on phones. Earbuds in. Strangers in proximity. When you use someone's name — the barista, the neighbor, the person your friend just met — you're creating a fabric of acknowledgment. You see people. They see you. That fabric makes the whole environment harder for someone who needs darkness to operate.

Small interruptions matter. Checking in matters. Asking "How do you two know each other?" isn't interrogation — it's interest. Humans who are present with each other, who notice each other, who stay connected — that's the friction.

None of this requires you to spot a predator or call one out. It just requires you to stop running the Docile Code that says *don't make it awkward, don't intrude, don't stay too long.*

Be awkward. Intrude a little. Stay.

THE NEW OPERATING SYSTEM

The predator's fatal error is assuming his target is an isolated node. He doesn't see the root system.

Women are not isolated nodes. They are a connected network — and it's activating.

Like mycelium — the fungal threads connecting trees underground, exchanging nutrients and warnings across entire forests — women are building digital root systems. Whisper networks like "Are We Dating the Same Guy?" now connect 3.5 million women sharing data instantly. Touch one node, activate the entire system.

The predator doesn't see the Standing Army of protective fathers we built the case for earlier — men realizing their job isn't just to protect their own daughters, but to change the environment for everyone.

And he doesn't see the technology dismantling his Silence Code.

Project Callisto solved the Prisoner's Dilemma — the "his word against mine" isolation that kept survivors silent.

It's a matching escrow: Survivor A files a confidential report. Nothing happens. Until Survivor B names the same offender. Then both connect. Survivors report three times faster. They're five times more likely to come forward when they know they aren't alone. The Silence Code requires isolation. Technology is eliminating that variable.

When we stay connected — presence, names, interest, networks — we aren't hunting predators. We're just being humans who see each other.

And that's enough to crash the code.

Rachael Denhollander wasn't the Wrong Woman because she became a lawyer. She was the Wrong Woman because she was an empowered human who chose to grow into someone who could dismantle the entire ecosystem. The predator's algorithm couldn't predict who she would become.

Here's what the algorithm can't compute now: with the network activated, every woman is the Wrong Woman.

The scan was built for isolated targets. That era is ending. Touch one node, and you activate all. His vulnerability scan returns zero reliable results—because no one is truly alone anymore.

The code is obsolete. There's nowhere left to run.

CHAPTER EIGHT

CHANGING THE MEDIA NARRATIVE

The Legacy Code Glitch

"Women who have an experience that legally would be rape instead label what happened to them as 'miscommunication.'"
Professor Heather L. Littleton

When I examine the media landscape, I don't see bad people or lazy writers. I see an industry running on *Legacy Code*.

Anyone who's worked in software knows Legacy Code. It's the system that still runs, still matters, but was built on outdated frameworks with varying documentation. The original developers are long gone. Nobody quite understands why it works the way it does. It's clunky, prone to bugs, and resistant to change—but we keep using it because it's what we've always done. Legacy Code carries weight. It shapes many things built on top of it.

For decades, Hollywood's Legacy Code for "high stakes" drama has been sexual violence—the rape or disempowerment of a female character to glorify, celebrate, or motivate a male hero. There's a name for this glitch: *Fridging*.

The term comes from *Green Lantern #54* (1994), where the hero Kyle Rayner returns home to find his girlfriend Alexandra DeWitt murdered and stuffed into a refrigerator. Comic writer Gail Simone later cataloged the pattern on her 1999 website "Women in Refrigerators"—documenting over 100 female characters killed, raped, or depowered purely as plot devices for male protagonists.

Fridging is lazy, sexist writing for four reasons. First, the victim exists only in relation to the male hero—a "sexy lamp" that could be replaced by an inanimate object. Second, while male characters die in stories too, female characters face domestic assault, sexual violence, and death for shock value at vastly disproportionate rates. Third, the trope reinforces that women are objects to protect or damsels to rescue. Fourth, the narrative focuses on the *man's* emotional trauma and revenge—the woman's murder doesn't propagate her story; it jumpstarts his.

The data confirms the pattern. Eighty percent of TV shows contain violence, according to EBSCO Media Research. Ninety percent of assault perpetrators know their victims— yet media consistently depicts stranger attacks, according to NSVRC. We've copy-pasted this code for so long we've forgotten we can write something else.

I'm not here to shame the people running the old system. I'm here to offer an upgrade.

BUTTER VS. THE CHAIN: A CASE STUDY

To understand the difference between Old Code and New Code, compare two productions fifty years apart.

The Old Code: *Last Tango in Paris* (1972)

Director Bernardo Bertolucci and Marlon Brando conspired to assault their lead actress on camera. The scene: Brando's character uses a stick of butter to simulate anal rape of the character played by nineteen-year-old Maria Schneider. The detail was not in the script. Schneider was not informed.

Bertolucci later admitted he wanted "her reaction as a girl, not as a prepared actress." He sought genuine rage and humiliation. He got it.

"I felt humiliated and, to be honest, I felt a little raped, both by Marlon and by Bertolucci," Schneider said in interviews. "After the scene, Marlon didn't console me or apologize."

Schneider never did another nude scene. In interviews over the years, she spoke publicly about struggling with drug addiction following the film—an experience that significantly impacted her life. She died in 2011.

When Bertolucci's admission resurfaced in 2016, the industry responded. Jessica Chastain wrote: "To all the people that love this film—you're watching a 19-year-old being violated by a 48-year-old man. The director planned her attack." Chris Evans added: "They should be in jail."

The system used her trauma as raw material. That's a bug, not a feature.

The New Code: *Normal People* (2020)

The Hulu series features a sex scene between Connell and Marianne that runs nine minutes and twenty-four seconds—one-third of the episode. It is intimate, raw, and undeniably hot. It is also a masterclass in consent.

The dialogue: "Is that okay?" and "If you want to stop, we can stop… it won't be awkward." They discuss contraception and virginity naturally, without killing the mood.

This wasn't improvised. It was choreographed by Ita O'Brien, a pioneer in the Intimacy Coordinator field. Actors Paul Mescal and Daisy Edgar-Jones praised the process—it "took pressure off completely" and "never felt clinical or creatively dead."

The result? A cultural phenomenon. "The Connell Effect" launched an Instagram account and a boom in silver chain sales. The show proved that consent doesn't kill the mood—it *makes* the mood. Actors went deeper because the safety net was there. Audiences felt that safety, and the heat went viral.

THE INTIMACY COORDINATOR REVOLUTION

The role of Intimacy Coordinator existed in theater for decades, but gained Hollywood traction after #MeToo. In 2018, actress Emily Meade requested a neutral party to supervise sex scenes on HBO's *The Deuce*—following allegations against a co-star. HBO responded by becoming the first studio to require Intimacy Coordinators for all productions with intimate scenes. Netflix, Hulu, Starz, and Amazon followed by 2020.

Here's the P&L on that decision.

In 2020 alone, twenty-three Emmy-nominated programs credited Intimacy Coordinators—including *Euphoria*, *Watchmen*, and *Succession*. These shows proved you can tell gritty, adult stories while maintaining the Safety Code on set.

The revolution expanded. *Sex Education* on Netflix built its entire premise around teaching consent—Ita O'Brien coordinated. *I May Destroy You* on HBO explored the gray areas of consent and healing—actress Weruche Opia used a body double for one scene, an example of protocols working exactly as designed. *Bridgerton* put female pleasure front and center with choreographed intimacy, not improvisation.

By February 2024, SAG-AFTRA formalized the standards. Their "Standards and Protocols for Use of Intimacy

Coordinators" made the key principle contractual: informed, continuing consent is now a requirement, not a courtesy.

There are now fifty to one hundred trained Intimacy Coordinators working in Hollywood. Pioneers like Ita O'Brien and Alicia Rodis—who co-founded Intimacy Directors International and consulted with SAG-AFTRA on the protocols—have professionalized what used to be "figure it out in the moment."

We used to throw actors into a bed and tell them to improvise, giving them no greater respect than stunt performers get for a car chase—actually, less. Stunt coordinators have existed for decades. Now, intimacy gets the same treatment.

This isn't about policing content. It's high-performance production. Consent wins awards.

THE AI FRONTIER

Just as we're fixing the code in Hollywood, new malware has hit the server: AI deepfakes.

In January 2024, AI-generated explicit images of Taylor Swift flooded X, racking up forty-five million views in roughly seventeen hours before removal. The images originated from a Telegram group using Microsoft's Designer tool. One woman's face was weaponized at scale, without her knowledge or consent.

This is Fridging gone algorithmic. The obsession with violation has shifted from the writer's room to the machine. It removes the human element entirely—the ultimate objectification.

The statistics are staggering:

- 96–98% of all deepfakes are non-consensual pornography

- 99% of victims are female

- 464% increase in one year

- 8 million projected in 2025 — up from 500,000 in 2023

- Nearly 4,000 female celebrities catalogued on deepfake porn sites

The crisis isn't limited to celebrities. In August 2024, South Korea faced an epidemic: teachers and female students victimized by deepfake images circulated via Telegram. Over two hundred schools were affected. By September 2024, South Korea had logged more than eight hundred deepfake sex crime cases—up from 156 in 2021.

In the United States, multiple high schools reported incidents—Aledo, Texas in 2023, and cases in New Jersey that same year. The victims were teenagers, and the perpetrators were often classmates.

The legislative response came. The TAKE IT DOWN Act

was signed on May 19, 2025—the first major U.S. law to substantially regulate AI-generated intimate imagery. Key provisions:

- Criminalizes non-consensual intimate imagery (NCII), including AI deepfakes

- Requires platforms to remove content within 48 hours of notice

- Penalties up to two years imprisonment (three years when minors are victims)

- Platforms must establish notice-and-removal processes by May 19, 2026

The bill passed the House 409-2. Near-unanimous, bipartisan support. When the violation is this clear, even Congress can agree.

We've moved from watching assault depicted in movies to generating assault via AI. The Carbon Copy fascination with violation has found its most scalable form. This is why we need the Consent Code embedded in law, not just culture.

THE VIEWER'S VOTE: DELETE, EDIT, SAVE

We are the end users. We control demand. We don't need to yell at the screen. We just need to run our own code.

DELETE: If a show hooks you with lazy trauma porn in the first ten minutes, that's the Old Code trying to keep you engaged. Turn it off. Refuse to validate the legacy system with your viewing time.

EDIT: Notice the Fridging. When you see it, name it: "That's Old Code." Once you can identify the manipulation, you stop buying into it.

SAVE: Champion the evolved stories. Watch the shows that hire Intimacy Coordinators. Support narratives built on connection, agency, and consent. The industry follows the audience.

If we demand evolved storytelling—stories where women are architects, not collateral damage—the factory will build it.

Let's watch *that* show.

CHAPTER NINE

WITCHES OF THE PAST; WHORES OF TODAY

Malware Code of the Silenced "Whore"

"When a woman thinks alone, she thinks evil."
The Malleus Maleficarum (1487)

In the 1600s, mass witch hunts swept across Europe and Colonial America, driven by religious fervor, societal anxieties, and misogyny. Tens of thousands were accused, with thousands executed, primarily by burning at the stake. Germany's Würzburg trials and Norway's Finnmark trials were notable examples. Fueled by fear, accusations, torture, and the belief that witches harmed people and challenged divine order by entering into an unholy pact with the devil, women—especially those who were independent, elderly, or who violated traditional gender roles—were the main targets.

History repeats itself, though rarely in the same guise. *Have the burning stakes of the 1600s disappeared?* Ordinarily, we'd say yes. In reality, the stake hasn't disappeared; it has gone digital.

In the 1600s, women who challenged the power structure, especially by engaging in doctrinal heresy, were burned at the stake. That was the *hardware*. Today, we don't use fire; we use servers. The execution is no longer physical, but the operating system running the show hasn't changed in 500 years. The core thesis is confirmed by the data. To justify her removal from society, as soon as a woman challenges power, she is branded a *"Witch"*—which translates to "she is crazy"—or a *"Whore"*—which connotes "she is a liar." The strategy remains remarkably consistent. The Witches of that era have simply transformed into the Whores of today. Men, it seems, must burn women. No longer able to burn bodies, they've found cannon fodder in the victims of their unbridled lust, branding them whores and burning them at the stake of public shaming.

The witch trials weren't about witches. They were about women who refused to comply. Healers, midwives, the outspoken, the sexually autonomous, and the economically independent—these were the women accused of witchcraft and executed. Today, in the perception of patriarchal society, those same women are called whores, gold diggers, attention seekers, and liars. The *nominal labels* have changed, while the *functional labels* have not.

The pattern: *Woman challenges male power — Woman is labeled witch or whore — Label delegitimizes her claim — System destroys her credibility — Other women learn to stay silent.*

Here's the insight: "Witch" and "whore" are not descriptions of behavior—they are mechanisms of control. They serve as the *delete* command for women who threaten the operating system.

The European witch trials (1450-1750) weren't about supernatural beliefs; they were a systematic campaign to eliminate women who held social, economic, or healing power outside patriarchal control. Brian Levack's *"The Witch-Hunt in Early Modern Europe"* and Anne Barstow's *"Witchcraze"* document the scale: 40,000-60,000 executions out of 90,000-110,000 accused and tried. 75-80% of those executed were women. This wasn't random persecution—it was a targeted elimination of female power.

The demographics tell the story. The women were older, largely post-menopausal. Widows and unmarried women were heavily overrepresented. Healers, midwives, herbalists—women with some form of medical knowledge. Women sufficiently outspoken to be branded "quarrelsome" or "scolding" for daring to challenge the status quo. Women accused of sexual impropriety or autonomy for owning their bodies.

The code: A *Witch* was a woman operating outside male control. The accusation had nothing to do with actual supernatural beliefs. It was a label applied to women who threatened patriarchal economic, medical, or social authority.

THE SOURCE CODE: MALWARE FROM 1487

To understand the modern *Whore* label, you have to look at the original source code. It comes from the *Malleus Maleficarum* (1487), the primary manual for witch hunters. Written in Latin, the Malleus was first submitted to the University of Cologne in Germany on May 9th, 1487. The title translates as *The Hammer of Witches*. Written by Heinrich Kramer and Jacob Sprenger, it remained in use for three hundred years, wielding tremendous influence in the witch trials in England and on the continent. It served as a judicial case-book for the detection and persecution of witches, specifying rules of evidence and the canonical procedures by which suspected witches were tortured and put to death. Thousands of women were judicially murdered as a result of the procedures described in this book, for no other reason than a strange birthmark, living alone, mental illness, cultivation of medicinal herbs, or simply because they were falsely accused.

The manual explicitly states: "All witchcraft comes from carnal lust which is, in women, insatiable."

And then the full codification of female nature as inherently evil:

"All wickedness is but little to the wickedness of a woman. What else is woman but a foe to friendship, an unescapable punishment, a necessary evil, a natural temptation, a desirable calamity, a domestic danger, a delectable detriment, an evil of nature, painted with fair colours!"

The Malleus wasn't religious doctrine; it was an instruction manual for destroying women. Do not overlook the insight here. The concept of "Witch" was never about magic in the first place. The real reference was to uncontrolled female sexuality and presence. If a woman chose to own her own body, she was considered dangerous. If she challenged authority, she was a threat. If she sparked feelings in others—let's label that presence dangerous.

This is the exact root of the modern "Whore" label. The word has roots in Old English and Germanic languages, deriving from a term that initially meant "friend" or "dear one," but evolved to become a highly derogatory term related to female promiscuity. In Old English, it appeared as *hōre*, already meaning "prostitute" or "adulteress"—a descriptive, though not complimentary, term. The derogatory force intensified over centuries. The spelling with "wh-" appeared in the sixteenth century, even as the modern pejorative meaning became intertwined with Western culture's aversion to female sexuality outside of marriage—a standard different from what is applied to men. Today, "Whore" is a deeply offensive label used to denigrate women based on moral judgments about perceived promiscuity, whether or not it involves financial exchange.

The witch hunters also had physical enforcement technology: the *Scold's Bridle*. A cruel iron device used from the 16th to 19th centuries in Europe to punish women deemed verbally unruly or gossipy, it featured a headpiece with a metal plate that was forced into the woman's mouth to press down on the tongue, often with a spike to inflict pain and prevent speech. The headpiece enclosed the head with hinges to open and close, and a padlock at the back. The wearer was led through town, often attached to a chain, to publicly parade their punishment and humiliation. It was primarily used against women accused of nagging, gossiping, or "scolding," but also for slander or witchcraft accusations. It silenced the wearer by making speech impossible or extremely painful.

The Scold's Bridle has evolved into *the Non-Disclosure Agreement*. The NDA is the paper version of the Scold's Bridle—a legal device designed to hold the tongue. The bridle turned *"women should not speak"* into physical reality. The NDA turns it into legal reality. The pain of speaking trained women to self-censor. It still does.

MODERNIZING BURNINGS AT THE STAKE

We've substituted *burning bodies* with *burning reputations*. It has become an industry. The system doesn't attack the facts; it attacks character. It runs a predictable algorithm that sorts women into three buckets for the barely concealed purpose of destroying their credibility: the "Whore" label, the "Crazy" label, and the "Liar" label.

THE "WHORE" LABEL: SHE WANTED IT

The most efficient way to dismiss a woman is to weaponize her sexuality against her. If she is overtly sexual, she simply cannot be a victim.

Monica Lewinsky was Patient Zero of the internet age. A 22-year-old White House intern's relationship with the President became public knowledge. She was labeled *tramp, tart, slut, whore, bimbo, stalker*. His dismissive reference: *That woman.* Later, she was labeled *fame-seeking* and *opportunist.* The personal cost: two decades of public humiliation, contemplation of suicide, and an inability to work in her field. Her name became a punchline. She only recently reclaimed her narrative through anti-bullying advocacy.

The reframe was unambiguous. It stemmed from the power differential: she was 22, he was the President. She bore the *whore* label while the powerful man remained *the President.* As she noted, public humiliation is now a *commodity,* and shame is an *industry.*

The code: *Burn the woman's reputation to save the man's power.*

Bill Cosby's defense employed the same code. Accused by over 60 women of drugging and sexual assault—eventually convicted in 2018, then set free purely on procedural grounds in 2021—the defense admitted to giving women Quaaludes but framed it as a perk for "party girls." Quaaludes, chemically known as methaqualone, were a popular sedative-hypnotic drug prescribed for insomnia and anxiety in the mid-20th century, known for their strong depressant effects and high potential for abuse, leading to widespread addiction. The underlying code is powerfully insidious: if she likes to party—if she's a "Whore"—she has forfeited her right to boundaries. It effectively argues that "bad" girls do not have rights to their own bodies.

THE "CRAZY" LABEL: SHE'S UNSTABLE

If the "Whore" label won't stick, or if the woman is professionally accomplished, the system switches to "Crazy."

In 1991, Anita Hill testified before the Senate Judiciary Committee that Supreme Court nominee Clarence Thomas had sexually harassed her when she worked for him at the Equal Employment Opportunity Commission (EEOC)— the federal agency responsible for enforcing workplace discrimination laws and handling harassment complaints. The irony was brutal: the man accused of harassment had been leading the agency tasked with preventing it. Hill was instantly labeled. Journalist David Brock coined *a little bit nutty and a little bit slutty*. Senator Orrin Hatch suggested "erotomania." Thomas was confirmed 52-48. Hill's credibility was destroyed in real-time on national television.

The playbook is clear: You don't have to disprove the assault if you can label the woman "unstable." The long-term impact, though, was that EEOC sexual harassment claims doubled in the year following her testimony, while "The

Year of the Woman" (1992) saw record numbers of women elected to Congress.

Decades later, in 2018, Dr. Christine Blasey Ford, a psychology professor, testified that Supreme Court nominee Brett Kavanaugh had sexually assaulted her when they were teenagers. She was labeled *confused, mixed up, politically motivated* — modern synonyms for the "hysteria" label used in witch trials. Worse, the toll was severe. Ford received death threats, was forced to move four times, required a security detail, and couldn't resume her university teaching position for an extended period. She would later require a crowdfunding campaign of over $600,000 just to keep her safe. Kavanaugh was confirmed 50-48.

THE "LIAR" LABEL: SHE WANTS MONEY

When a woman cannot be portrayed as crazy or promiscuous, the system defaults to "Gold Digger." The assumption is that a woman only speaks up as a means to profit.

Even Rachael Denhollander—the first woman to publicly accuse Larry Nassar, launching the story into the national spotlight through an *Indianapolis Star* article in 2016—faced this dilemma. Despite 156 women testifying, Michigan State's Interim President's internal communications suggested Denhollander was likely receiving a "kickback" from trial lawyers.

She survived the Label Machine because her professional credentials (law degree) gave her standing, meticulous documentation kept for 16 years, and her *respectable* presentation as a conservative Christian married mother, along with 155 other women corroborating her claims. The judge called her the "Five-Star General" of the case.

The lesson: Even when a woman *wins*, the requirements are extraordinary. A law degree. Sixteen years of documentation. 155 corroborating witnesses. The burden of proof for women remains astronomically higher than for men. The math is brutal: it took 60+ women to convict Bill Cosby—and even then, the conviction was overturned. One woman equals dismissible. Sixty women equals maybe credible. **Notice what's never on trial: his consent practices.**

Kesha faced a similar legal battle. Between 2014 and 2016, when she sued producer Dr. Gottwald alleging years of sexual, physical, verbal, and emotional abuse and sought release from her recording contract, she was instantly labeled: *fabricating claims to get out of contract, money-motivated, career manipulator.* The judge denied her release. Kesha broke down sobbing in the courtroom. She was forced to continue working with her alleged abuser or not work at all. Often, settlement discussions hinge on the woman issuing a public apology—forcing her to brand *herself* a liar to gain her freedom.

Perhaps the most terrifying evolution from stake burning to digital burning: Amber Heard. In her 2022 defamation trial against Johnny Depp after she wrote an op-ed about being a domestic violence survivor, she was labeled *crazy, psycho, gold digger, liar, manipulator, Amber Turd.* It was a classic study in viral humiliation. The trial rapidly devolved into viral entertainment. Pro-Depp content dominated TikTok. Domestic violence organizations reported that survivors were afraid to come forward after witnessing her treatment.

This wasn't just public opinion—it was algorithmic execution. A report by Bot Sentinel found that nearly 25% of anti-Heard accounts were created in the prior seven months: bots and trolls using intentional misspellings to manipulate algorithms. The burning was automated. A purchased consensus.

THE REFRAME: FUNCTION OVER DESCRIPTION

We need to stop listening to the words and start looking at the function. When a man calls a woman a *whore*, he isn't describing her sex life. He is deploying a misogynistic weapon to revoke her right to consent. When the media calls a woman *crazy*, they aren't offering an expert diagnosis of her mental health. They are running a well-worn script to destroy her credibility.

If you're keeping score, that is seven major public burnings cited in fewer than 800 words: Lewinsky, Cosby's victims, Hill, Ford, Denhollander, Kesha, and Heard. We didn't even have to open the history books.

The labels function; they do not describe. Here's the translation guide:

When You Hear	The Function	Ask Instead
"Attention seeker"	Dismiss her testimony	What did she report?
"Gold digger"	Dismiss financial claims	What is she owed?
"Liar"	Dismiss her account	What's the evidence?
"Crazy" / "Hysterical"	Dismiss as mentally unstable	What prompted this label?
"Slut" / "Whore"	Dismiss as deserving it	Did he get consent?

PREEMPTIVE CREDIBILITY DESTRUCTION

"What evidence exists either way?"

In this season of the *Consent Code*, we must retire the "Whore" label just as we've retired the "Witch" label to the dustbin of history. It is not a descriptor of a woman; it is a weapon wielded by a man. The stake is gone. Now we must delete the code.

THE LABEL MACHINE: REWRITING THE CODE

The label machine has been running for 500+ years. It's time to run a system diagnostic.

Command: Run system diagnostic

Detected Malware: Label_Generator.exe

Origin: 1487 (Legacy Code)

Function: Automatically converts "Woman Challenging Power" into "Discredited Object"

Action Required: Execute Rewrite

DELETE — THE OLD CODE

IF woman_challenges_power = TRUE

THEN RUN label_generator.exe:

SELECT FROM [Witch, Whore, Crazy, Liar, Gold Digger]

APPLY label

EXECUTE credibility_destruction

OUTPUT: "She is the problem."

END IF

EDIT — THE TRANSLATION LAYER

The old code runs automatically, below conscious awareness. The edit installs a pause—a moment to recognize the pattern before reacting.

WHEN label IS DETECTED:

PAUSE reaction

RUN translation_protocol:

IF label == "Whore" THEN TRANSLATE TO "She owns her sexuality."

IF label == "Crazy" THEN TRANSLATE TO "She is reacting to gaslighting."

IF label == "Gold Digger" THEN TRANSLATE TO "She is demanding what she is owed."

IF label == "Liar" THEN TRANSLATE TO "Her truth is dangerous to his power."

OUTPUT: "The label is a weapon, not a descriptor."

SAVE — THE NEW CODE

The new code doesn't just defend against the label machine— it installs a different operating system entirely. One where intuition is a feature, not a bug. Where voice is protected, not punished.

INSTALL: Sovereign_Protocol.v1

DEFINE Intuition AS "biological_threat_detection"

DEFINE Voice AS "system_feature_not_bug"

DEFAULT SETTING: Believe the pattern, not the PR.

STATUS: Protected.

The witch trials ended. The word "witch" became a Halloween costume. But the function never died—it just migrated to new labels. Now it's our turn to make "whore" what "witch" has become: a relic of a brutality we no longer tolerate.

The stake burned bodies. Servers burn reputations. Same operating system. Time for a new one.

Delete the malware. Save the new code. Protect the protocol.

CHAPTER TEN

THE DISARMED OFFICER

The Arrest Gap and the Math That Breaks the System

"Law enforcement agencies were using the prearrest charge evaluation process as a means of screening out cases that were felt to be problematic... This has led to changes in the arrest standards used by police to bring charges, from 'one of probable cause' to 'proof beyond a reasonable doubt' to convict."
Office of Justice Programs (OJP), "Policing & Prosecuting Sexual Assault: Inside the Criminal Justice System"

I am not here to bash the police. In fact, I spend pro bono hours trying to add value to law enforcement. I've sat with officers. I've listened to their frustrations. I've seen what they're up against.

I need to state my position clearly because the cultural reflex is to blame officers for the dismal clearance rates in sexual assault cases. We look at the statistics and assume the officer who took the report pre-judged the victim, didn't believe her, was lazy, or didn't care.

Those situations absolutely exist. I've seen them. I've heard them. Even in Northwest Arkansas. But that's only part of the story—and very rarely is laziness or lack of care the root cause. More often, it's someone trying their best in a brutally difficult situation with inadequate tools.

When you examine the operational reality, something far more systemic emerges. We hired men and women to be protectors. We gave them a badge and asked them to stand between us and the wolves. Then we systematically stripped them of the power to do their job. We buried them in paperwork, hamstrung them with obsolete laws, and turned them into historians of crime rather than its problem-solvers.

This chapter is a defense of law enforcement against the system that employs them. Officers aren't failing victims. The architecture is failing officers. And perhaps a clearer architecture will help put into perspective the few mindsets that do need to change—around prejudgment, around believing victims, and around the victim-blaming patterns we explored in earlier chapters. When the system works, the outliers become visible. Right now, the system failure is so total that it obscures everything.

THE ARREST GAP: 50 VERSUS 90

Here is the math that breaks everything.

To make an arrest, an officer legally needs *Probable Cause*. In plain terms, that means roughly 50% certainty that a crime was committed. It's a "fair probability" standard. That's the law.

To convict at trial, a jury needs *Proof Beyond a Reasonable Doubt*. That's approximately 90% certainty. That standard exists because we don't want to imprison innocent people. It's the highest bar in our legal system, and it belongs in the courtroom.

The problem is that officers have been forced to meet the 90% courtroom standard before they can even make an arrest at 50%.

The Office of Justice Programs documented this precisely: law enforcement agencies began "using the pre-arrest charge evaluation process as a means of screening out cases," which "led to changes in the arrest standards used by police to bring charges, from 'one of probable cause' to 'proof beyond a reasonable doubt.'"

Yet nationally, rape cases are cleared by arrest at just 32.9%—already below the probable cause threshold—while officers are simultaneously expected to pre-litigate at 90%. The gap isn't 40 points; it's nearly 60.

Read that again. Officers on the street, in the immediate aftermath of a reported assault, are being asked to predict whether a jury will convict in three years. They're not asking, "Do I have probable cause to arrest this guy?" They're asking, "Will a prosecutor take this case? Will a jury believe her?"

That 40-point gap between 50% and 90% is where predators live. It's where cases die. I call it *The Arrest Gap.*

To understand the scope, look at the full hierarchy of legal standards: Reasonable Suspicion sits at roughly 42% certainty—enough to stop and question. Probable Cause is approximately 50%—enough to arrest. Preponderance of Evidence is 54%—the civil court standard. Clear and Convincing reaches 73%—used in some civil matters. Beyond Reasonable Doubt approaches 90%—the criminal conviction threshold.

An officer witnessing a sexual assault in progress has the legal authority to arrest at 50%. But because prosecutors are overwhelmed and juries are skeptical of "he said, she said" cases, officers have subconsciously adopted what researchers call a *Downstream Orientation.* They're not policing the crime; they're pre-litigating the trial.

The result is predictable. Of every 100 reported rapes, approximately 18 lead to arrest. Another 42 cases languish as "inactive" investigations. Roughly 30 are cleared through "exceptional clearance"—a designation that often means the case was closed without an arrest, frequently not in accordance with federal guidelines. Fewer than 7 result in conviction.

Officers have the handcuffs, but the system has tied their hands.

THE DOWNSTREAM ORIENTATION PROBLEM

Why does this happen? Because officers learned—through experience, through departmental pressure, through watching cases collapse—that arrests without "perfect" evidence create problems.

Section 1983 of the Civil Rights Act allows citizens to sue officers for civil rights violations. An officer who arrests someone later found innocent can face personal liability. Departments, seeking to minimize lawsuits, began requiring officers to seek prosecutor approval before making arrests in sexual assault cases—even though no law requires this step.

This creates an informal elevation of the standard. Officers aren't asking, "Did a crime occur?" They're asking, "Can I prove it to a prosecutor's satisfaction right now, on this street, at 2 AM?"

The OJP study found that cases involving alcohol, non-stranger assault, or perceived "risky behavior" by the victim were being "screened out at street level." Not because officers didn't believe the victims, but because officers knew those cases wouldn't survive the downstream gauntlet.

We built a system that punishes officers for acting on probable cause. Then we blamed them for not acting.

THE PAPERWORK PRISON

The administrative burden has turned protectors into data entry clerks.

According to the Bureau of Justice Statistics, less than 10% of a patrol officer's on-duty time is spent on crime-related activities. A 2019 Nuance Communications report found that 56% of law enforcement professionals spend over three hours per shift writing reports or documentation. Some estimates place average administrative time at 40-50% of total duty hours.

Picture this: You hire a Navy SEAL. You train them in tactics, strategy, and confrontational combat. You hone their instincts through grueling preparation. Then you assign them to a desk and tell them their primary job is transcribing "he said, she said" dialogue into a database for eight hours a day.

That's modern policing.

No one puts on a uniform because they have a passion for filing. They do it because they are passionate about protection. We've taken our most expensively trained human assets—people with the instinct to hunt predators—and converted them into glorified secretaries for a broken judicial system.

The caseload crisis compounds this. At the Sex Crimes Unit of the Philadelphia Police Department, 60 investigators handle 4,100 cases. That's 64 cases per investigator—thirteen times the typical homicide caseload. The Police Executive Research Forum has noted that sex crime investigations require "time and painstaking work, but budgets and manpower are inadequate."

Officers aren't lazy. They're drowning.

THE "ROMANCE NOVEL" REPORT

The first step in any sexual assault investigation is the responding officer's written report. What officers include—and how they word it—shapes every downstream decision.

A National Institute of Justice study analyzed more than 5,600 police reports from 1993 to 2011 using machine learning techniques. The finding was disturbing: sexual assault reports often read less like criminal investigations and more like relationship dramas.

Reports focused on relationship dynamics rather than consent mechanics. Phrases like "no bruises," "known prostitute," "prior relationship," and "alcohol involved" appeared without an explanation of their legal relevance.

The linguistic signaling of officer attitudes toward victim credibility—conscious or not—affected case outcomes.

This isn't malice. It's a failure of framework.

Consider a bank robbery. We don't ask if the teller had a prior relationship with the robber. We don't note whether she had been drinking before she was held at gunpoint. We ask about the mechanics of the crime: How did the robber gain entry? What did he take? How much?

But because officers haven't been given a clear *Consent Code* to investigate, they default to assessing "vibes." They describe whether the victim seemed credible rather than documenting the specific mechanics of how consent was or wasn't obtained.

Asking a patrol officer to analyze the nuances of a toxic relationship without a clear legal definition of consent is like asking a plumber to perform heart surgery. It's not their job, and it's unfair to expect it.

MORAL INJURY: THE WOUND THEY DON'T TALK ABOUT

We discuss post-traumatic stress in law enforcement. PTSD is the psychological consequence of what officers see—the violence, the death, the human wreckage.

There's another wound. It's called *Moral Injury*, and it's the trauma of what officers *couldn't do*.

Moral Injury is not a theory. It is a clinically documented psychological phenomenon. The term originated in military psychiatry to describe the deep psychological damage that occurs when a person is forced to act—or prevented from acting—in ways that violate their core moral beliefs.

For law enforcement, it manifests when an officer's identity as a *protector* is obstructed by the system they serve.

The FBI Law Enforcement Bulletin states it directly: "If officers cannot save a gravely injured victim at the scene of a crisis, they may feel like failures. As a result, they may blame themselves and experience feelings of guilt, frustration, and shame."

A study published in PMC (PubMed Central) found: "When police officers' action plans, or willingness to help those who suffer, are precluded or not completed successfully, then officers may experience moral distress. The ongoing experience of moral distress may lead to compassion fatigue, which may eventually lead officers to experience PTSD."

This is the part that breaks my heart. An officer stands in front of a victim. Every instinct says *protect.* The victim is telling the truth—the officer knows it in their gut. But the law in their state requires "forcible compulsion" before a rape charge can be filed.

No external bruising? No weapon? No visible injury?

The officer cannot make an arrest.

They have to look at that victim and say, "There's nothing I can do."

That moment—repeated across thousands of cases, in hundreds of departments, over years of service—creates deep soul wounds. It goes against every biological and professional imperative of someone who signed up to protect. It is, in the most literal sense, a systemic castration of the protective instinct we need most.

Officers carry this burden. They don't talk about it. Many don't have the language for it. But Moral Injury is real, it is measurable, and our system is inflicting it on the very people we've asked to stand between us and harm.

THE ARKANSAS EXAMPLE

Take my home state of Arkansas.

Arkansas law requires "forcible compulsion" for rape charges. That means if a woman was coerced, manipulated, or froze in fear—but wasn't externally beaten black and blue or threatened with a weapon—an officer is legally powerless to make an arrest.

The biological freeze response, documented extensively in trauma research, is not recognized as evidence of non-consent. The victim's nervous system protected her by immobilizing her, and the law treats that immobilization as ambiguity.

An officer in Arkansas can interview a victim, believe every word she says, know with moral certainty that a crime occurred—and still have to walk away because the statute says "no force, no crime."

But here's what else is true about Arkansas: It's where Walmart, Tyson, and J.B. Hunt were built. Northwest Arkansas has one of the highest concentrations of entrepreneurial energy in America. We disrupt Fortune 500 supply chains from strip malls in Bentonville.

If we can build that, we can rewrite a criminal code. The entrepreneurial infrastructure is already here. It just needs a new target.

RE-ARMING THE PROTECTOR

We don't need to "defund" the police. We don't need to lecture officers about trauma-informed interviewing. They know the job. What they need is the framework to do it.

Technology that frees their eyes. Officers need transcription tools that handle documentation so they can stay present with victims and vigilant on the street. We need AI that creates immutable chains of custody—so "he said, she said" becomes "the transcript said." We need systems that reduce the 3+ hours of paperwork per shift to minutes, returning that time to actual protection. The tools exist, and some of these tools focus on the officer as the user experience (e.g. CLIPr). The question is whether departments will deploy them.

Legal standards that match reality. Officers need laws that clearly define consent—so they're investigating consent mechanics, not relationship drama. They need statutes that recognize the freeze response as evidence, not ambiguity. They need probable cause to mean probable cause again.

Ecosystem changes that empower protection. When Detroit finally tested 11,341 backlogged rape kits, they identified 841 serial predators. One-third of offenders were serial—triple the rate visible in court records. Testing those kits didn't just bring justice to old cases. It prevented future ones. That's what happens when we build systems that support officers instead of burdening them.

DELETE. SAVE

This chapter is a defense brief.

Delete the assumption that officers don't care. Most signed up to protect. The system converted them into historians of human misery.

Delete the downstream orientation. Probable cause is 50%. Build the ecosystem that lets officers act on it.

Delete the paperwork prison. Technology exists to handle transcription. Deploy it.

Save the Protective Energy. Officers—regardless of gender, department, or jurisdiction—carry the instinct to stand between the vulnerable and the wolves. That energy is not the problem. The framework is.

To every officer who has stood in front of a victim, knowing the truth but unable to act: We see you. We know you didn't sign up to file reports while predators walk free. You signed up to stop them.

We're here to help build the system that lets you.

CHAPTER ELEVEN
THE MISSING CODE

Why the Men We Love Need Structure, Ritual, and Challenge

"Young men need structure. They need ritual. They need challenge. When we take those away without replacement, we don't get healthier men — we get lost ones."
Scott Galloway

With this chapter, we arrive at a pivotal moment. We are calling out what has happened—and what is still happening—to the men we love: our brothers, fathers, coworkers, partners, friends, husbands, and boyfriends. These men have not abandoned their protective instincts. They want to show up. They want to speak up when and where it matters. But something has gone wrong in the system that was supposed to develop them.

And here is a truth we must be willing to say out loud: much of this comes from us. The women who love these men have told them, again and again, "Don't do anything about it." Not because we don't want them to protect, but because we are terrified of losing them. We have watched the news. We have seen what happens when someone intervenes and it goes wrong. We have imagined the phone call, the hospital, the funeral. And so we have said, "Please, just stay out of it. I need you here. I need you alive." Our fear—born from love—has trained the men we love to stand down. We have demasculated them with the best of intentions.

We have moved from a "Protective Community" model to an "Isolated Agency" model. We have eliminated the structures that once taught young men how to channel their energy. We have pathologized competition, sanitized play, and digitized connection until what remains is a generation of men who are—in the language of researchers—"digitally dominant but socially submissive." They can dominate a screen but struggle to engage in person.

This is not a character indictment. This is a systemic failure.

The data is stark. Sixty-three percent of men under 30 are single, compared to 34% of women in the same age range. Thirty percent of men aged 18-30 report zero sexual partners in the past year—up from 8% in 2008. Young men are spending seven or more hours per day on screens. The average age of first romantic encounter has climbed. These are not lazy men. These are men who were never given the guidance they needed.

Scott Galloway has been sounding this alarm for years. Young men need structure—a framework that tells them where to put their energy. They need ritual—repeated practices that build identity and belonging. They need challenge—something difficult that forges capability and confidence. When we eliminated these without building replacements, we didn't create a safer generation; we created a lonelier one.

The answer is not to shame them. The answer is to rebuild what we broke.

THE SPACES WE NEED TO PROTECT

This means protecting spaces where men compete, struggle, and develop together: gyms, sports leagues, and yes, even fraternities—not because they're perfect, but because the structure isn't the problem. The code running inside the structure is the variable. A fraternity running Legacy Code produces cover-ups and conspiratorial silence. A fraternity running Consent Code produces accountability and protectors. We've been trying to delete the container instead of updating the software.

The same principle applies to sports teams, military units, religious communities, and every other space where men gather. When the code says "protect each other from consequences," you get cover-ups. When the code says "protect the community from harm," you get men who show up.

This means encouraging play. Rough-and-tumble energy isn't disorder—it's development. Boys who wrestle learn boundaries. Boys who compete learn resilience. Boys who lose learn recovery. When we pathologize this energy instead of channeling it, we don't eliminate it; we just ensure it has nowhere healthy to go. And when energy has nowhere healthy to go, it finds somewhere unhealthy.

Young men are starving for initiation. They're finding it in online communities that radicalize them, in algorithms that feed them rage, and in influencers who sell them dominance fantasies disconnected from responsibility. The answer isn't to eliminate their hunger for belonging; the answer is to feed it with something that actually works.

This means gyms. This means competition. This means challenge. Not because we want to return to some imagined past, but because these spaces do something that screens cannot: they build men in the presence of other men. They create accountability through witness. They channel energy into growth rather than consumption.

THE BIOLOGICAL REALITY

I am not going to pretend biology doesn't exist.

Testosterone levels in American men have declined roughly 1% per year since the 1980s. A 2021 study from the University of Miami, Northwestern, and the University of Manitoba—sampling over 4,000 men ages 15-40—found that mean testosterone levels were significantly lower in 2011-2016 compared to 1999-2000. The decline persisted even among men with a normal BMI. This is not simply an obesity story.

A 2025 meta-analysis in the Journal of Endocrinological Investigation went further. Analyzing over 1,200 papers and more than a million subjects, researchers found a statistically significant negative correlation between testosterone levels and year of measurement. More critically, they found that LH (luteinizing hormone)—the brain's signal to produce testosterone—is also declining. The authors describe this as a "resetting of hypothalamic-pituitary-gonadal function."

Something environmental is affecting the hormonal command center. Endocrine disruptors in plastics, pesticides, and personal care products are prime suspects. Men's bodies are being chemically reprogrammed to produce less of the hormone historically associated with drive, risk-taking, and protective behavior.

I state this not to excuse behavior or to claim that low testosterone causes predation. Predators exist at every testosterone level. I state it because we must acknowledge the full picture. We are asking men to show up while the biological infrastructure is being quietly degraded. The answer is not to throw up our hands; the answer is to recognize that what biology may be taking away, community and ritual can restore. Structure, challenge, and competition naturally support healthy hormonal function. The gym is medicine. The team is therapy. The ritual is restoration.

THE INDUSTRIAL SHIFT

To understand how we arrived here, we must understand what we lost.

The male breadwinner model feels ancient. It isn't. It emerged during the Industrial Revolution—roughly 150 years ago—when factories pulled men out of homes and villages and into wage labor. Before that, in most subsistence economies, protection and provision were distributed across the community. Multiple adults watched multiple children. Work and home were integrated. Men were present.

Industrialization created the "separation of spheres"—men in factories, women in homes. It isolated the protective function into a single node: the father. And it made that node responsible for everything. Provider. Protector. Disciplinarian. All of it, alone.

That model was always precarious. Now it is collapsing. Blue-collar men have seen their share of household income fall from 75% to 64% between 1985 and 2018. Marriage rates have declined alongside the decrease in working-class men's relative earnings. Counties affected by manufacturing job loss show men with higher rates of depression, suicide, and social withdrawal.

We built an economic system that told men their worth was measured by their paycheck. Then we eliminated the jobs that provided those paychecks. Then we wondered why men were disappearing.

The breadwinner model was never the "traditional" human arrangement. It was a 150-year experiment that is now failing. What came before it—distributed protection, community responsibility, men developing alongside other men—is actually older and more natural. We are not proposing something radical. We are proposing a return to something that worked.

THE ECONOMIC CASTRATION

Before we continue, I need to address the "Deadbeat Dad" narrative—because it is part of how we have removed men from the communities that need them.

There are $32 billion in unpaid child support arrears in America. Only 43-44% of custodial parents receive the full support owed. The cultural story is that non-paying fathers are monsters who abandon their children.

The data tells a different story.

A California study found that 76% of the $14.4 billion in arrears was owed by parents who *lacked the ability* to pay. The median income of these "deadbeats" was $6,349 per year. Their median arrears were $9,447. Seventy-one percent of support orders were set by default—meaning the parent wasn't even present at the hearing.

Nationally, 80% of those in arrears have annual incomes below $20,000. Sixty percent earn below $10,000.

This isn't deadbeat. This is broke.

When a man cannot provide—when the system sets support orders he mathematically cannot meet, then jails him for non-payment, making him even less employable—we have removed another node from the protective network. We have taken someone who might have been present for his children and converted him into a fugitive from a system designed to produce failure.

We need men in the community, not exiled from it. The family court system, as currently constructed, often accomplishes the opposite of its stated intention. It doesn't create more support for children. It creates more absent fathers.

THE SILENCE THAT DEAFENS

On August 22, 2025, Iryna Zarutska—a 23-year-old Ukrainian refugee who had fled war seeking safety in America—was stabbed to death on a Charlotte light rail train. She remained conscious for nearly a minute after the attack.

I will not condemn the bystanders in that train car. A man with a knife who has just killed someone is not a situation where intervention is reasonable to expect. That is survival instinct, not cowardice.

What I will address is what happened *after*.

The media barely covered it. A young woman—a refugee, someone who came to this country believing it was safe—was murdered in public, and the story cycled out of the news within days. We have extensive coverage of celebrity controversies. We have minimal coverage of a systemic failure that left a woman bleeding out on public transportation while her attacker, a man with 14 prior arrests, was free to board that train.

The silence is the symptom. When we don't talk about these failures, we can't learn from them. When we can't learn from them, we can't update the code. North Carolina did pass "Iryna's Law" (House Bill 307), adding "committing a crime on public transportation" as a sentencing aggravator. That is something. But it is reactive, not preventive. It addresses punishment after the fact, not presence beforehand.

We must be willing to look at what is happening. We must be willing to say it out loud. The men we need cannot develop if we refuse to acknowledge the stakes.

THE INFRASTRUCTURE OF SHOWING UP

Good Samaritan laws exist in all 50 states. They are designed to protect people who help in emergencies from being sued for unintentional harm. In theory, this should encourage intervention.

In practice, the laws say "you MAY help without penalty" rather than "you SHOULD help." Only three states—

Minnesota, Vermont, and Rhode Island—actually require bystanders to provide reasonable assistance. In the other 47, intervention is legally framed as optional.

The result is predictable. Only 40% of people who experience out-of-hospital cardiac arrest receive bystander help before professionals arrive. Yet when bystanders do act, survival rates double or triple. The gap isn't character—it's confidence. Less than 5% of Americans receive formal CPR training each year.

Here is the proof that this is infrastructure, not character: States that invest in training see dramatically different outcomes. Alaska has a 79.7% bystander CPR rate. Nevada hits 57.5%. Oregon reaches 54.6%. Same Americans. Different training. Different expectations. Different code installed.

When you train people, fund programs, and create an expectation of intervention, people intervene. When you leave safety to chance and individual heroism, you get inconsistent coverage at best.

This is what we mean by rebuilding the code. It is not about hoping men will magically become protectors. It is about building the systems—the gyms, the teams, the training, the rituals, the expectations—that produce men who show up.

THE FRAMEWORK FOR INTERVENTION

For those who want to show up but don't know how, the framework already exists. It's called the 5 D's—originally developed by Green Dot and expanded by Right To Be:

Direct: "Hey, is everything okay here?" Straightforward engagement when you feel safe to do so.

Distract: Spill a drink. Ask for directions. Pretend to know one of them: "There you are! I've been looking for you." Interrupt the dynamic without direct confrontation.

Delegate: Get help. "Can you call security?" Tell a bartender, a bouncer, an RA, a host. Use authority figures when you need backup.

Delay: If you can't intervene in the moment, check in afterward. "Are you okay? Do you need a ride home?" Showing up doesn't have to be instantaneous.

Document: If other interventions aren't possible, record what's happening. Note details for a potential report. Create evidence.

The key principle: Intervene at the earliest point possible. Don't wait for certainty—ambiguity is precisely when you should act. Curiosity is a superpower. When something feels off, get curious. Ask questions. Create friction. Most predatory behavior relies on bystander passivity. The moment someone pays attention, the dynamic shifts.

THE NETWORK WE HAVE

There are 72-75 million fathers in America. Fifty-seven percent consider parenthood "extremely important" to their identity. This is the largest untapped network for cultural change in the country.

Here is what we know about fathers: CEOs with daughters hire more women and pay them better. A father's presence correlates positively with his daughters' resilience. When men have proximity to vulnerability—when they are connected to people who need them to show up—their behavior changes.

This is not abstract. This is architecture. When a man is clear about his own boundaries, present in his community, and connected to people who depend on him, he becomes exactly what we need: someone dangerous to predators because he refuses to look away.

The men we love are not broken. They are missing the code that tells them where to go and what to do when they get there. We can install that code. We can rebuild those structures. We can create the gyms, the teams, the rituals, and the expectations that develop men who show up.

DELETE. SAVE.

Delete the isolated breadwinner model. It was a 150-year experiment. It failed. Protection was never meant to be one man's burden.

Delete the "deadbeat" narrative that exiles men from their children. The data shows most aren't refusing—they're struggling financially. Keep men in the community.

Delete the pathologizing of competition, play, and challenge. These are the forges that build men. Protect them.

Save the spaces where men develop together. Gyms. Teams. Fraternities with updated codes. Challenge, ritual, and structure.

Save the expectation that men show up. Train them. Fund the programs. Build the infrastructure. Make intervention the norm, not the exception.

Save the 75 million fathers who are waiting to be activated. Give them a role. Give them a code. Give them something to protect.

To every man reading this: You are not lost. You are not broken. You are not the problem.

You are the solution we haven't deployed yet. The code is missing. Let's write it together.

CHAPTER TWELVE

THE ACCOUNTABILITY GAP

When Leaders Look Away

"Too many people in power knew about the behaviors and the complaints, and yet the predators continued on the payroll and abused even more students."
U.S. Department of Education Finding, Larry Nassar Investigation

Here is the math that should keep every leader awake at night.

At Penn State, by 2002, at least twelve people knew about Jerry Sandusky's abuse of children: three senior administrators, including the president and vice-president; legendary head football coach Joe Paterno; a graduate assistant who witnessed the assault directly; that assistant's father; multiple campus police officers, including a detective who was told to close his investigation; two janitors; their supervisor; and the CEO of The Second Mile charity. Twelve people. Zero action. Sandusky continued abusing boys for another nine years.

At Michigan State University, the pattern repeated—but worse. They had the Penn State playbook. They watched that institution hemorrhage $109 million in settlements and suffer a complete leadership purge. And still, when Amanda Thomashow reported Larry Nassar's abuse in 2014, the university sided with Nassar. They concluded his "pelvic floor" treatments were "medically appropriate." They let him return to treating patients. The Title IX coordinator even called his methods a "liability" that exposed patients to "unnecessary trauma"—and still, no one acted.

The final cost: $500 million from MSU alone. Another $380 million from USA Gymnastics. $138.7 million from the FBI for mishandling the case. Over one billion dollars total. 332 survivors. And in a detail that should end any remaining faith in institutional self-correction: Dean William Strampel, the man responsible for overseeing Nassar, was himself convicted of felony misconduct for sexually harassing students. The person tasked with investigating abuse was also an abuser.

This is the Accountability Gap: the distance between knowing and acting, between awareness and intervention, between the leaders we need and the leaders we have.

In tech, when a system is riddled with bugs, you do not just patch it—you look at the architecture. At scale, individual bugs are rarely isolated mistakes. They are symptoms of fundamental design flaws. The standard root-cause analysis approach shifts the question from "Who wrote this bad code?" to "Why did the architecture allow this error in the first place?" The same framework applies here. Sandusky was not a bug. Nassar was not a bug. They were symptoms of an institutional architecture designed to protect the brand while leaving people inside uncertain. The failure is not a bug. It is a feature.

THE MINIMUM VIABLE SEARCH

Let me tell you about a search that never happened.

In 2017, Alexander Acosta was nominated to be the United States Secretary of Labor—the department responsible for combating human trafficking. A basic search of his professional history would have revealed that in 2008, as U.S. Attorney for the Southern District of Florida, Acosta had approved a non-prosecution agreement for Jeffrey Epstein. The deal allowed the most notorious sex trafficker of our generation to plead guilty to lesser state charges, serve 13 months in a county jail with 12-hour work-release privileges, and—critically—receive immunity from all future federal prosecution for himself and his co-conspirators. The deal was hidden from Epstein's victims, violating the Crime Victims' Rights Act.

This was not secret information. It was in court records. It was in news archives. A docket search with keywords like "Epstein" or "sex trafficking" would have surfaced it immediately.

And yet.

Acosta was confirmed. He served as Labor Secretary for two years before resigning in 2019 amid renewed scrutiny. In 2020, the Justice Department's Office of Professional Responsibility concluded that Acosta used "poor judgment" in negotiating the agreement and failing to notify victims. A federal judge ruled that he and his team had violated the Crime Victims' Rights Act.

The question is not why Acosta did what he did. The question is: Where were the journalists? Where were the Senate staffers doing opposition research? Where were the advisors whose job it is to vet nominees? Where was the minimum viable due diligence that would have surfaced a federal prosecutor's "sweetheart deal" with a pedophile?

The vetting void is not about missing information. The information was there. The vetting void is about a system that does not prioritize looking.

This is the same pattern that let Sandusky continue for sixteen years—before a mother finally wouldn't let it go. The same pattern that let Nassar continue until a hundredth gymnast came forward. The same pattern that allows predators to operate in plain sight while institutions choose not to see.

THE ARCHITECTURE OF LOOKING AWAY

Dr. Jennifer Freyd has spent over thirty years studying why institutions fail the people they are supposed to protect. A professor emerita of psychology and lifelong activist against sexual violence, Freyd founded the Center for Institutional Courage and introduced the concepts that now define this field: institutional betrayal, institutional courage, and DARVO—the pattern of Deny, Attack, Reverse Victim and Offender that institutions use to deflect accountability.

Her central insight is this: Institutions do not accidentally fail. They are architecturally designed to protect the brand while leaving the people inside uncertain. The failure is not a bug. It is a feature.

Institutional betrayal, Freyd argues, occurs when an institution fails the very populations it should protect— ignoring reports, silencing survivors, and prioritizing reputation over truth. This betrayal compounds the original trauma. Survivors are harmed not just by the perpetrator but by the system that was supposed to help them.

The antidote is what Freyd calls Institutional Courage: an institution's commitment to seek the truth and engage in moral action, despite unpleasantness, risk, and short-term cost.

This is not abstract philosophy. Freyd has operationalized it into concrete steps—a protocol for leaders who want to close the Accountability Gap. These are her 12 Steps of Institutional Courage:

- Comply with criminal law

- Comply with civil law

- Respond sensitively to victim disclosures

- Bear witness—acknowledge harm publicly

- Apologize for harm caused by institutional failures

- Take steps to prevent future harm

- Conduct anonymous surveys to identify misconduct

- Cherish the whistleblower

- Commit to transparency

- Ensure leadership accountability

- Democratize decision-making

- Address root causes, not just symptoms

The first two steps are baseline, not ceiling. If your institution is debating whether to meet legal minimums, you have already failed.

Rachael Denhollander, the first to publicly accuse Larry Nassar, said it plainly: "Had MSU apologized to survivors and listened to them about reforms, many would not have sued." The heartbeat of most survivors is simple: "I just don't want to see this happen to anyone else." Leadership thought only in terms of liability—and paid five times more than Penn State as a result.

THE ECOSYSTEM PROBLEM

Dr. Se Youn Park, a feminist security studies scholar at the University of Queensland, has been asking a question that most institutional leaders avoid: What happens when the problem is not one institution, but an entire ecosystem?

Park's research focuses on digital sexual violence—crimes like South Korea's Nth Room case, where a network of Telegram chatrooms was used to blackmail and sexually exploit women and girls. Her central argument is that these crimes are not individual acts by individual predators. They are modular, scalable, and global. They are enabled by platform architectures that facilitate distribution, monetization, and anonymity.

Park argues that platforms are not "passive hosts." They are infrastructures that make certain crimes possible. And infrastructures have leaders. Someone is making decisions about what gets built, what gets monitored, and what gets allowed.

This matters for institutional leaders because the ecosystem is shifting. Your institution does not exist in isolation. The codes that govern your workplace intersect with the codes that govern platforms, law enforcement, legal systems, and cultural norms. A leader who understands only their own organization will be blindsided by systemic forces they never saw coming.

Park's framework—treating digital violence as an ecosystem problem rather than an individual problem—is the same framework we need for institutional leadership. The question is not just "Who is the bad actor?" The question is "What architecture allowed this to happen, and who is responsible for that architecture?"

THE GLOBAL SHIFT TO PREVENTION

The legal code is catching up.

The UK Worker Protection Act 2023, effective October 2024, mandates that employers take "reasonable steps" to prevent sexual harassment rather than just responding after it happens. The emphasis is on proactive duty. Employers cannot wait until an incident occurs. If they breach this duty, tribunals can increase compensation by up to 25%. The Equality and Human Rights Commission can take enforcement action against organizations that fail.

This is the paradigm shift: from individual perpetrator to system failure, from response to prevention, from reaction to architecture.

In the United States, states like California now require employers to establish written Workplace Violence Prevention Plans. The focus is shifting from "Who did this?" to "Why did the system allow this?"

This is the new standard. Leaders who are still operating in a reactive mode—waiting for incidents, managing liability, prioritizing brand protection—are running outdated code. The law is moving toward prevention. The culture is moving toward accountability. Leaders who do not move with it will find themselves on the wrong side of history and the wrong side of the settlement table.

DELETE. SAVE

Delete the self-preservation code. Remove the architecture that prioritizes institutional reputation over truth. It is malware. It will cost you more than it saves.

Delete the vetting void. Build systems that search, that surface, that flag. If a basic docket search would reveal the problem, conduct the search.

Delete the reactive mindset. The law is shifting to prevention. The culture is shifting to accountability. Shift with it or be left behind.

Save Dr. Freyd's Institutional Courage protocol. Compliance is the floor, not the ceiling. Bear witness. Acknowledge harm. Cherish the whistleblower. Address root causes.

Save the ecosystem awareness. Your institution exists within systems. Understand those systems. Take responsibility for what your architecture enables.

Save the leadership standard that actually leads. Not the version that hides behind legal disclaimers. Not the version that manages liability while predators operate. The version that stands in the gap. The version that acts when twelve people know and no one else will.

The Accountability Gap does not close itself. It closes when leaders decide to close it.

The question is whether you will.

CHAPTER THIRTEEN

SYSTEMIC RE-EMPOWERMENT

Installing the Antivirus

"Freedom would be meaningless without security in the home and in the streets."
Nelson Mandela (1995 Freedom Day)

Twelve chapters of diagnosis. We have named the malware. We have traced the source code from its Latin root to the courtroom, from the choking epidemic to the accountability gap, from the predator's algorithm to the institutions that enable its existence. We have stared at the 975 cases that exit the system for every 25 that lead to a jail cell. There is a justified right to anger here.

This chapter is not about anger. This chapter is about architecture.

The tone shifts here—from the heavy *what's broken* into the vibrant and operational *what works*. This is not about more rules. It is about better infrastructure. It is about creating a world in which the default setting is safety, so that the end result can be unfettered joy. We are not here just to survive. We are here to thrive, to connect, and—quite frankly—to experience more of the kind of intimacy that makes life worth living.

But to arrive at that place, we have to re-empower the systems that hold us together. We must move from a "Risk Management" mindset to a "People Protection" mindset. And we have to start with proof that the upgrade actually works.

THE PROOF OF VELOCITY

If, even for a moment, you think the system is too big to change, go back to Chapter Four. The Take It Down Act was signed into law on May 19, 2025. It passed the House 409-2 and sailed through the Senate unanimously—bringing together legislators who often cannot agree on anything. It embedded consent infrastructure directly into the operating system of the internet by mandating that platforms remove non-consensual images within 48 hours.

That happened in under two years. From a viral incident in a Texas high school to a federal law with criminal penalties. That was not a ceiling. That was a floor.

The question we now ask our legislators is simple: we updated the code for AI-generated images in two years. Why are we still using 1980s rape statutes for human beings?

THE GLOBAL BLUEPRINT: SWEDEN AND THE NEGLIGENT RAPE STANDARD

We do not have to guess whether affirmative consent works. We just have to look at the data from countries that have already implemented the patch.

In July 2018, Sweden enacted the *samtyckeslagen*—the Consent Law. The shift was fundamental. Under the old code, proving rape required evidence of violence, threats, or exploitation of a vulnerable state. The new law moved the entire legal framework from "No means No" to "Only Yes means Yes." Under this model, all sexual acts require clear and active consent. If consent is not given, the act is a crime—regardless of whether force was involved.

The results were immediate and measurable. In 2017, the year before the law, Sweden recorded 190 rape convictions. By 2019, that number had risen to 333—a 75 percent increase in convictions over two years. This increase was not due to more people committing assault but because the legal system finally had the language to address what was already happening.

But Sweden went further. They added a layer of accountability that directly addresses the problem we have faced for decades—the "he said, she said" friction where a perpetrator can claim they "thought" it was fine. Sweden's solution was a new legal category called *Negligent Rape*.

Here is how it works: Negligent rape applies when consent is unclear, and the perpetrator failed to take the necessary step to clarify it. You may not have intended to commit rape, but you did not check. The law holds you accountable for that failure to verify. In 2023, Swedish courts processed 26 negligent rape cases, and every single one resulted in a conviction.

Read that again. Not because the number is large, but because the conviction rate is absolute. When the legal standard shifts from "did she fight back?" to "did he verify?" the ambiguity collapses. The message becomes operationally clear: if you are unsure, you check. If you don't check, you are liable.

Sweden was not the only country to take action. Since 2018, sixteen European Union member states have adopted consent-based definitions of rape, including Belgium, Denmark, Finland, Germany, Greece, Ireland, the Netherlands, and Spain. Iceland, Norway, Switzerland, and the United Kingdom also employ consent-based frameworks. In late 2025, France's Senate voted 327-0 to adopt a consent-based rape definition—triggered by the Gisèle Pelicot case, which made global headlines and forced the nation to confront its legal framework.

We already know this works closer to home. As we discussed in the Introduction, New Jersey has required "affirmative and freely-given permission" since 1992. Their rate: 17 per

100,000—less than half the national average. Colorado implemented the same update in 2022 and saw a 26 percent decrease in cases within two years.

The code works. The patch is available. The question is not whether to install it but why we are still running the old version.

THE BUSINESS CASE: CONSENT AS A PROFITABILITY MULTIPLIER

If you are a leader, an operator, or a CFO, I want you to stop thinking of consent as an HR liability and start viewing it as a profitability multiplier.

The data is not subtle. McKinsey's research, tracking over a thousand companies across fifteen countries, found that companies in the top quartile for gender diversity on executive teams were significantly more likely to outperform on profitability than those in the bottom quartile. That correlation has strengthened with every study they have published—from 2015 through their most recent 2023 report. The Peterson Institute for International Economics, analyzing nearly 22,000 firms across 91 countries, found that moving from 0% to 30% female representation in the C-suite is associated with a roughly 15% increase in profitability for a typical firm. The driver was not board seats. It was women in operational leadership—the CFOs, the COOs, the people making daily decisions.

And here is what makes the data personal. Among the S&P 500, female CEOs make up roughly 6% to 8% of the total. Yet over a ten-year period, the companies they lead have dramatically outperformed their male-led counterparts on stock returns. The sample is small. The gap is not.

Why? Because feminine leadership is not just about representation. It is about a collaborative intelligence that breaks down the silos of proprietary information and replaces them with a shared, transparent operating system. When a workplace lacks a clear Consent Code, employees spend a significant portion of their energy on threat detection—scanning for predatory behavior, navigating unwritten rules, protecting themselves from risk managers who care more about the company's reputation than its people. That is wasted processing power.

When you install safety, you unlock innovation. The equation is simple: Safety plus psychological security equals better decisions equals better business.

This is not a moral argument dressed in business language. This is the business argument on its own terms. Consent infrastructure is a competitive advantage. The companies and institutions that implement it first will outperform those that don't.

BENDING THE SYSTEM TO THE BODY

For too long, we have designed our systems for male convenience. I invite you to consider the eternal, yet interrupted, wisdom of childbirth.

For thousands of years, women gave birth upright—standing, squatting, kneeling. Using gravity, rhythm, and the wisdom of their own bodies. Upright positions are documented throughout history in ancient, medieval, and indigenous cultures. They are physiologically advantageous. Gravity aids the descent of the baby. The pelvic outlet opens wider. Labor is shorter. The body knows what it is doing.

Then the Reference Man walked into the room.

You met him in the Introduction—the architect behind the crash test dummy that was built for his body, not hers. Here, he appears as the early male physician who decided that the procedure of childbirth was easier for *him* if the woman lay flat on her back. Better view for the observer. Worse outcome for the participant. He turned a powerful biological act into something done *to* a woman rather than *with* her.

That same philosophy found its way from the labor room into the courtroom. Our legal system embodies the "lying flat" position of justice. It requires victims to be passive, to be observed, and to prove they were "forcibly compelled" to fight against a system that does not understand their biology. The woman's body freezes during an assault—a survival mechanism called tonic immobility—and the system interprets that as a lack of resistance.

Systemic Re-Empowerment means we stop asking the body to bend to the system and start bending the system to the body. We need laws that recognize the frozen response for what it is: a biological survival mechanism, not evidence of consent. We need a system that stands upright—proactive, affirmative, and honoring the intuition of the person in the room.

ONE PERSON CAN CHANGE THE CODE

If you still feel that one person cannot change anything, let me tell you about Chanel Contos.

In February 2021, Chanel was twenty-three years old, living in London, and studying for her Master's degree. She was not a politician, not a lawyer, not a lobbyist. She was a young Australian woman who noticed a pattern among her friends—stories of sexual assault that kept surfacing quietly in private conversations that never went anywhere.

She posted one Instagram story. One question. She asked her followers if they, or someone close to them, had been sexually assaulted while at school.

Within 24 hours, 200 people responded yes.

Chanel did not stop. She launched a website—teachusconsent.com—and a petition calling for holistic consent education in Australian schools. Within weeks, 44,000 people had signed. Nearly 7,000 people submitted anonymous testimonies of sexual assault. The New South Wales Police launched a collaborative operation with Chanel that resulted in a 54 percent increase in sexual assault reporting in a single month. State after state began announcing consent education mandates—Victoria, New South Wales, Queensland, each moving independently because the momentum was undeniable.

Then, on February 17, 2022—exactly one year after that first Instagram story—education ministers from every state and territory in Australia unanimously agreed to mandate consent education in every school, from foundation through Year 10, effective 2023.

One person. One question. One year. An entire country's code, updated.

Chanel herself has said that she knew so little about the system that nothing scared her. The naivety that might have stopped someone else became the superpower that allowed her to walk into rooms with ministers and commissioners and say what 50,000 petition signers needed her to say. She was not an expert. She was an activated human who refused to accept that the system was too big to change.

Today, Teach Us Consent has expanded beyond Australia. Chanel runs the Centre for Sex and Gender Equality at The

Australia Institute, was named one of the BBC's 100 most influential women, and published her book *Consent Laid Bare* through Harper Collins. Her latest campaign, Fix Our Feeds, is taking on algorithmic consent—calling for opt-in features on social media platforms.

I tell you this story not because Chanel is exceptional, but because she is replicable. One question, asked with clarity and courage, in the right moment and to the right audience, can activate a network that was already waiting to be activated. The code was ready for the update; she just (expertly) pressed install.

THE NEW DEFAULT

In 1969, a young medical researcher named Dr. Sonnet Ehlers was on call when a rape survivor walked into her ward. The woman looked at her and said, "If only I had teeth down there." Dr. Ehlers made a promise that night. Forty years later, she delivered on it — selling her house and car to fund Rape-aXe, a female condom lined with jagged, teeth-like hooks that latch onto a perpetrator during an assault and can only be removed by a physician. She designed it with engineers, gynecologists, and psychologists, and consulted convicted rapists to understand whether it would make them rethink their actions. She distributed 30,000 during South Africa's World Cup.

I am pretty unbothered about the tools in my arsenal, and this one is no different. Dr. Ehlers gave us the most literal version of the new default: before you engage, you had better be confident that consent has been given — because the body's architecture can now respond. This is not a threat; it is a design. Think of it like any other safety protocol: you do not climb into a car and hope the brakes work. Consent is how you confirm the mechanism is off.

This is not about fear; it is about the basic operational awareness required for a high-performance interaction.

HAVE MORE SEX. HAVE MORE SPACE

This chapter has been about installing the antivirus. But prevention is only half the mission. The other half — the half that matters most — is what becomes possible when the malware is gone.

When we create safe spaces, we are not creating sterile environments. We are creating the foundation for high-enthusiasm intimacy. When we are no longer afraid, we are free to be curious. We can explore the warmth of feminine energy and the strength of masculine presence without the malware of shame or the fear of violation.

The antivirus is not the destination; it is the infrastructure that makes the destination reachable. And the destination is joy, connection, and play — the kind of intimacy that requires two people who are fully present, fully choosing, and fully alive to each other.

Sweden installed the patch and saw more justice. Companies that implemented safety measures saw more profit. Australia installed consent education in under a year because one person asked one question. The code works; the proof is in.

We are building a world that is safer, more profitable, and — if we do this right — a lot more fun. Welcome to the new operating system.

CHAPTER FOURTEEN

THE NEW CODE

Your Personal Consent Toolkit

"You do not rise to the level of your goals. You fall to
the level of your systems."
James Clear, Atomic Habits

The architecture is built. Chapter Thirteen installed the operating system — proof that consent infrastructure works at scale, generates profit, and shows that one person with one question can update an entire country's code in under a year. Sweden moved. Australia moved. New Jersey has been running the patch since 1992. The system works.

This chapter puts the tools in your hands.

Not theory. Not statistics. Not another diagnosis. Sixteen codes — each designed to run on the infrastructure we just built. These are the commands you carry with you. Into a conversation. Into a bedroom. Into a bar. Into a boardroom. Into the rest of your life. A caring team has built, itemized, and packaged them for everyday use. Your only obligation now is to install them. Now is better.

1.   The Debugger: Delete. Edit. Save.

The core command sequence of the entire book.

DELETE the shame scripts, the obligation scripts, the "Perfect Victim" checklist that filters out too many cases. Delete the voice that tells a survivor it was somehow their fault. Delete the instinct to ask what she was wearing.

EDIT the question. Stop asking "Why did you go there?" and start asking "Who did this?" Stop asking "Why didn't you fight back?" and start asking "Why did he do this?" The edit is not cosmetic. It redirects the entire investigation — internal and external — from the person who was harmed to the person who caused the harm.

SAVE the new default: boundaries that honor your gut, communities that check in, laws that ask "Did she agree?" instead of "Did she resist?"

This is not a one-time decision. It is a practice. You train the debugger the way you train a muscle — repetition until the new pattern becomes automatic. The first few times you catch yourself running old code, it will feel clunky. That is the point. Awareness is the first rep. Keep going.

2.   The Check-In Ritual: "Still Good?"

Two words. Build them into the sequence until skipping them feels as wrong as driving unbuckled.

Consent is not the brakes. It is the engine. The brakes stop something. The engine is what makes the whole thing move. Without the check-in, you are coasting on assumption — and assumption is where every crash starts.

The Check-In applies everywhere: in the bedroom, at a party when your friend's eyes go glassy, in a meeting when a colleague is being steamrolled, at the dinner table when someone has gone quiet. "Still good?" is not a formality. It is an invitation. It opens a door and says: you can stay, you can leave, you can change the terms. Whatever your answer is, it matters to me.

Practice it until it becomes muscle memory. Not a thought experiment. Not something you do once to prove you are a good person. A reflex. Like checking your mirrors before changing lanes.

3. The Signal: One Finger, Two Fingers, Three

Sometimes words fail. The room is loud. The moment is charged. The words are stuck somewhere between your brain and your mouth because your body got there first.

One finger = Red. Stop. Two fingers = Yellow. Pause. I need to talk. Three fingers = Green. Go ahead.

No speech is required. Consent becomes visible. It works in dating, classrooms, workplaces, and parties. It removes the verbal barrier that keeps so many people locked in silence when their bodies are already screaming their answers. If the Consent Code is the software, this is one of the simplest pieces of hardware to run it on.

4.   The Carbon Copy

You are running scripts right now that you did not write. They were installed by your family, your culture, your peers, your media diet, and your fear. Most of them are invisible. Most of them are harmless. Some of them are not.

A Carbon Copy is any behavior you replicate without conscious choice. The way you greet people. The way you respond to authority. The way you say yes when your body is screaming no. It is the awkward hug you give on autopilot at a family gathering because the script says "be polite." It is the silence you maintain when someone makes a comment that makes your skin crawl, because the script says "don't make it weird." It is the automatic "of course!" to a favor you do not have the bandwidth for because the script says "don't be selfish."

None of these are choices. They are copies. And every time you run one in a small moment, you are rehearsing for the big ones. The script does not know the difference between a favor and a boundary. It runs the same subroutine whether the stakes are a family dinner or a locked bedroom door.

You are not broken. You are just running someone else's code.

5. The Carbon Copy Scan

Now that you can see the code, run the scan.

Pick one behavior this week and make it conscious. Just one. Before you react, pause and ask: "Did I choose this, or did I copy it?" If the answer is "I copied it," run the debugger. Delete it, edit it, or save it — but make it yours.

The scan is not a one-time event. It is a practice. The first few times you do it, it requires effort. Eventually, it becomes automatic — a background process running quietly while you navigate your day. You train the scan the way you train any habit: repetition until the conscious choice becomes the default.

Start small. The hug you do not want to give. The yes you do not mean. The laugh that covers your discomfort. Name it. Scan it. Decide if it stays or goes.

6. The Enter and Exit Framework

You cannot feel safe in a room if the door is locked from the outside.

Every interaction has an entrance and an exit. Explicitly open the container. Explicitly close it. Name what you want and need on the way in: "Tonight I need to feel heard. I need to be touched gently. I want to play. I want conversation before anything else." And when the landscape shifts mid-encounter — because it will — name that too: "I love the energy, but I need more space right now."

Name where you are on the way out. What felt good. What did not. What you would want different next time.

When the exit is visible, people stop scanning for danger and show up with their full attention. This applies to intimacy, dates, difficult conversations, and work meetings — any encounter where vulnerability is present. The container is not a cage; it is a frame. And when both people can see the frame, the picture inside becomes much more interesting.

7.   The Honest Itinerary

Before your next encounter — casual or otherwise — answer three questions. Out loud or on paper. Not in the vague privacy of your own head, where self-deception thrives.

First: What am I actually offering? Residency? A visit? One night? Exploration? Something I have not figured out yet? Be specific. Vagueness is where deception hides.

Second: What do I actually want from this? Connection? Release? Companionship? Validation? Fun? Something I am not ready to name? Be honest. With yourself first.

Third: Am I willing to say this out loud to the other person?

This is the gate. If the answer is yes, proceed. If the answer is no, you are not ready for the encounter. Not because your desires are wrong — but because the Consent Code requires honesty. If you cannot articulate what you are offering, you cannot obtain genuine consent for it. And if you are afraid to say it out loud, examine why. Is it shame? Address the shame, not the desire. Is it because they would say no? Then you do not have consent. Is it because you do not know? Get clear before involving someone else.

The Honest Itinerary is not a mood killer; it is the foundation that makes the mood trustworthy.

8. Resident vs. Tourist

Two valid relationship operating systems.

The Resident commits, buys property, learns the neighborhood, and invests in the long-term infrastructure of a shared life. The Tourist visits with great energy, appreciates the destination, and does not pretend the trip is permanent. The Tourist cleans up after themselves and leaves the destination better than they found it.

Both are valid. Neither is deception. The old code declared Residency the only acceptable operating system, which created shame around everything else. Shame produced deception. Deception causes harm. The friction was never about the lifestyle — it was about the lie.

The violation occurs when a Tourist pretends to be a Resident to get through the door. That is not tourism; that is fraud. And when a Resident secretly wishes they were a Tourist but stays out of obligation, that is a Carbon Copy running in the background — an inherited script that says, "this is what you are supposed to do," while the body quietly deteriorates under the weight of pretending.

Run the Honest Itinerary. Name what you are. Let the other person decide if they are open to that offer.

9. Enthusiasm Over Control

This is the diagnostic that separates healthy desire from predatory behavior. Write it down. Teach it to your kids. It changes everything.

The question is simple: Do I need my partner's enthusiasm to feel satisfied, or do I need their compliance?

If mutual excitement is what makes it good — if you need them present, responsive, choosing to be there — that is clean code. That is desire operating as it should.

If having power over someone is what makes it good — if their passivity, their confusion, their inability to resist is part of the appeal — that is predator code. And it does not matter how charming the delivery is.

The old code constantly confuses these two things. It tells young men that simply wanting sex makes them predatory. That is a lie, and it corrupts their programming. Desire is healthy. Pursuit is healthy. The distinction is mutuality. Play lives on enthusiasm. The Predator Code lives on control. One is the engine; the other is the malware.

10. The Courageous Conversation

Someone will tell you something happened to them. The old code wants to investigate. It wants to ask what they were wearing, whether they had been drinking, whether they "led them on." Delete that code.

Replace it with tender, attuned words: "I am so sorry that happened. What do you need right now?"

That is it. That is the entire protocol. You do not need to solve anything. You are not being invited into an adjudicatory role. You are not a detective. You are being called upon to be present — to hold space without filling it with your own discomfort. Curiosity is the antidote to victim blaming. Not the curiosity that interrogates, but the curiosity that asks what the person in front of you actually needs in this moment.

Most people who disclose trauma are not asking you to fix it. They are asking you to witness it. The courageous conversation is the one where you resist every urge to investigate, and you simply stay.

11. The Bystander Code: Five D's

The Green Dot Intervention Program, expanded by Right To Be, outlines the 5 D's as a well-respected, certifiable, trainable intervention framework. Five options at every comfort level:

Direct — "Hey, is everything okay here?" Step into the situation. Name what you see.

Distract — Create a reason to engage. Pretend to know them. Spill a drink. Ask for directions. Interrupt the dynamic without confronting it directly.

Delegate — Alert a host. Call security. Text a friend. Bring in backup when you cannot or should not intervene alone.

Delay — The Morning After check-in. You saw something, but the moment passed. Follow up with, "I noticed something last night. Are you okay?" Delay is not failure; it is the recognition that intervention does not expire.

Document — Record what you see. Quietly and accurately. Evidence is power, and sometimes the most important intervention is creating a record that exists if the survivor needs to use it.

The key insight: this is not about heroism. It is about training. States that invest in bystander training see dramatically different outcomes. The same people, different code installed. You do not need to be brave; you need to be prepared. The superpower that makes all five D's work is curiosity — when something feels off, get curious. That single instinct disrupts more predatory behavior than today's written policy.

12. The Community Care Antivirus

If Coercive Control isolates, Community Care connects. The predator's business model depends on disconnection. Your job is to make that model fail.

The Group Text Protocol: Friends going out designate an anchor. Agree on a signal and an exit plan before leaving the house, not after three drinks. The anchor is not the babysitter; the anchor is the person everyone checks in with — and who checks in with everyone. "You good?" is not nagging; it is the network running its scan.

The Host Alert: If you are hosting, you own the room. You set the tone. You redirect the predator's access without making a scene. You are not the bouncer; you are the firewall. The person lingering too long at the bar with someone who is clearly not engaged? That is your cue. Walk over, introduce yourself, and offer a drink. Interrupt the pattern.

The Morning After: One text message. "I noticed something last night. I care. You are not invisible." That text is worth more than you will ever know. It tells the person: you were seen. Someone was paying attention. You are not alone.

The predator cannot find a host when the whole community is running the same antivirus.

13. The Queen Code

Three and a half million women in "Are We Dating The Same Guy?" groups have made a personal decision to share what they know. Each one of those women chose — individually and autonomously — to participate in a distributed protection network. That choice is the Queen Code.

This is not about the network itself. The network is the infrastructure — the mycelium that connects root to root underground. The Queen Code is the personal decision to plug in. To stop keeping what you know to yourself. To share the information that keeps other women safe, even when the old code tells you to stay quiet, mind your business, or worry about being called "dramatic."

The Queen Code says: I have information that could protect someone, and I am choosing to share it. That is not gossip. It is not a whisper network born of fear. It is a Village Firewall built out of abundance. It is protected by Truth Defense and Anti-SLAPP laws. It is actions generated by an untouchable mass of the divine. And every time one woman plugs in, the entire system grows stronger.

You do not need permission to activate your Queen Code. You just need to decide that silence is no longer the default.

Early in this work, when I met certain survivors, my first thought was: *that man raped the wrong woman.* She was too smart, too connected, too resourceful. He picked the wrong target.

As I got deeper, something shifted. The Queen Code activated — not as theory, but as lived experience. I watched women plug into the network. I saw the divine and the Queen Code lines light up in real time. And my perspective changed completely.

All women are the wrong women to rape.

That is the Queen Code at full power. Not because every woman has a law degree or a platform, but because every woman who plugs in activates a system that makes the predator's cost of operation infinite. The network does not care about your resume. It cares that you exist. One node activates the whole system.

14. The Man Code

If you are a father of daughters, you will feel this in your bones — but fatherhood is not a prerequisite. This is not a "Dad Code." It is a Man Code.

Scott Galloway has been mapping this territory with precision. In *Notes on Being a Man*, he lays out a framework that is deceptively simple: Protect. Provide. Procreate. His argument is that healthy masculinity is not about dominance or emotional stoicism — it is about competence, surplus value, and showing up when things get hard. A man's default setting should be to protect. If he conflates being male with coarseness, bullying, predation, or abuse of power, he is not masculine — he is anti-masculine.

Galloway identified three things young men are starving for: Structure, Ritual, and Challenge. Structure tells them where to put their energy. Ritual gives them repeated practices that build identity and belonging. Challenge forges capability and confidence.

Here is what this book adds to that framework: Consent lives inside all three.

Ritual is where consent takes root. The repeated practices — the check-in before the moment escalates, the pause before the assumption, the question asked even when you think you know the answer — these are rituals. They are not compliance exercises. They are practices that build a man's identity as someone who shows up with awareness, not entitlement. Every time you run the "Still good?" check-in until it becomes muscle memory, you are creating a ritual that rewires your operating system.

Structure requires consent to function. You cannot invest your energy in a team, a relationship, a community, or a career without the ongoing agreement of the people in that space. Structure without consent is a cage. Structure with consent is architecture. When a man learns to seek consent for where he places his energy — rather than assuming his presence is always welcome — his energy becomes significantly more effective.

Challenge is where you pursue consent you want but do not yet have. The job. The relationship. The conversation you have been avoiding. The boundary you have been afraid to set. Consent is not just about sex. It is about the full spectrum of human negotiation — the ability to ask for what you want, hear "no" without crumbling, and return with a better offer. That is challenge. And it builds men who are dangerous to predators precisely because they have learned that rejection is not a wound — it is information.

Every man has a front door. Your protection extends from that door outward to every woman within your radius. If you are not a dad, consider the roles of uncle, brother, coach, or neighbor. Reset the Bro Code: move from conspiratorial nods to real questions — "What are you doing?" Model consent at home: when a child waves instead of hugging a relative, that is the Consent Code installed before the child even knows the word.

The Man Code is not an organization. It is a decision that "not her" means "not anyone."

15. The Arsenal: Tools for Physical Safety

I am unbothered about the tools in my arsenal. We live in a world with a physical imbalance, and the market has responded with more options than most people realize.

The biting condom analogy from Chapter Thirteen applies here at the personal level: proceed as if every safety mechanism is engaged until enthusiastic consent has been confirmed. That is the new default in every encounter.

But software updates need hardware to run on. The hiking stick with a concealed blade. The noise keychain. The stun gun. The flashlight with a knock-you-out handle. The personal alarm that is louder than your fear. There is no excuse for being unprotected anymore. The list goes on, and what follows is a catalog of the practical tools available to close the physical gap.

The Arsenal is not about living in fear. It is about living prepared. The woman who carries a personal alarm is not paranoid — she is proactive. She has assessed the environment, identified the gap between the code she wants to live by and the world she actually lives in, and she has closed it with hardware.

16. The Label Translator

You will hear them: gold digger, attention seeker, crazy, liar, slut. The labels arrive quickly, and the old code tells you to accept them at face value — to let the label replace the person.

The Label Translator installs a pause between hearing a label and reacting to it. One question: What is this label doing?

When you hear "gold digger," ask: "What is she actually owed?" When you hear "crazy," ask: "What behavior prompted this label?" When you hear "liar," ask: "What evidence exists either way?" When you hear "attention seeker," ask: "What did she actually report?"

Labels function; they do not describe. Every one of them is a code designed to short-circuit your curiosity and route you straight to dismissal. The Translator intercepts that code and forces you back into the question. It is a three-second practice that changes the entire trajectory of a conversation — and, often, of a case.

Delete the question "What kind of woman is she?" Save the question "Did he get consent?"

Run the debugger once this week. Pick one code from this chapter. Just one. See what happens.

Delete the obligation you have been carrying that was never yours. Edit the script you have been running on autopilot since someone else installed it. Save the boundary you have been negotiating away because the old code told you it was not worth the friction.

You were never a puppet. You were just running a carbon copy. Now you have the source code. And the source code says this: you get to decide what stays and what goes.

Everything is to your advantage. The law is moving. The data is in. The proof is in. Sweden installed the patch. New

Jersey has been running it for three decades. Companies that implemented safety saw more profit. Australia updated the code in under a year because one woman asked one question.

The code works. The proof is in. Now it is yours to run.

Have More Sex. Have More Safety. Have More Space. Welcome to the new codes.

FIFTY STATES. ONE CODE

The Movement Beyond the Manual

"The most powerful movements have always been built around what's possible, not just claiming what is right now. Trauma halts possibility. Movement activates it."
Tarana Burke, founder of the Me Too movement

The last chapter handed you a personal toolkit: codes you can carry in your pocket, load on your phone, and practice with the people closest to you. That chapter was about what one person can do. This closing is about what happens when we connect those individuals — communities, businesses, institutions, and legislators — and rewrite the rules we are all expected to live by.

We have moved beyond individual human ability now. What follows is about connected human ability.

THE GLITCH: YOUR ZIP CODE DETERMINES YOUR PROTECTION

Right now, the level of legal protection a woman receives when she reports a sexual assault depends almost entirely on where the incident took place. Not on what happened to her. Not on the evidence. On the zip code. Less than half of states even define consent. Half still require proof of force. In Arkansas, there is no statutory definition of consent, and prosecution requires proving "forcible compulsion." The burden falls on the person who was already violated to demonstrate that she resisted — physically, visibly, provably. We have skipped over every human step to ask a person being attacked to produce evidence of a struggle. That is the current code. That is what we are here to rewrite.

One solution: direct victims to leave more marks on their aggressors (that's dangerous). Our solution: change the codes to reflect human reality.

THE PROOF: IT WORKS WHEN YOU INSTALL IT

New Jersey has required "affirmative and freely-given permission" since 1992. Result: the lowest sexual assault rate in the nation. Colorado installed the same update in 2022, unanimously bipartisan — not a single dissent. Within two years, offense rates dropped twenty-six percent. Sweden reformed to affirmative consent in 2018; convictions rose seventy-five percent. France's Senate voted 327 to 0 for consent-based rape law. This is installed code producing measurable results. The only question is why the majority of American states are still running force-based statutes.

THE PROOF OF VELOCITY

The Take It Down Act passed the House 409 to 2, was unanimous in the Senate, and was signed into law in May 2025. Ted Cruz and Amy Klobuchar co-sponsored it. From a high school deepfake incident in Aledo, Texas, to signed federal law in under two years, it mandates platforms remove non-consensual images within forty-eight hours. If we can build consent infrastructure into the internet for AI-generated images, we can mandate it for human beings. That is the question we bring to every legislator: we updated the code for deepfakes. Why are we still running 1980s statutes for people?

THE CONTAGION MODEL

You have already met Chanel Contos. One person. One clear question. One viral trigger. One country's education system, updated. That is the model this book runs on. The code does not require a revolution. It requires a clear question, a brave voice, and a network ready to amplify.

You picked up this book. You are already part of the network. The question now is what you will do with it. You do not need to be Chanel. You need to be the person who asks, "Still good?" at the dinner table. The person who runs the

Label Translator when someone is dismissed. The person who texts, "I noticed something last night," the morning after. The mycelium does not need a hero. It needs nodes. And you are one.

THE MISSION: HMS

HMS is the engine behind this book — and the engine is running.

We are building a world where consent is law in all fifty states. Where sex is a conversation, not a crisis. Where every human being has the tools to connect on their own terms. We are rewriting criminal codes, training the institutions that failed us, and building a culture where enthusiastic consent is the baseline — not the exception.

It will be a long journey. So we intend to have more sex along the way.

Have More Sex. Joyful, shame-free, consent-forward, well-educated intimacy. When safety is the default, enthusiasm follows.

Have More Safety. Consent training frameworks for communities, law enforcement, universities, and institutions.

Have More Space. Consultation, technology products, and creative strategy for organizations ready to evolve.

VOLUME 2

This book is Volume 1. Volume 2 will incorporate codes submitted by readers, communities, and practitioners. Your codes. Your innovations. Submit them to hello@havemore. space. We are building this together.

THE NEW OPERATING SYSTEM

I started this book with a differentiation between "kind of human" and "human kindness." We are all the same kind of human. But human kindness is an active choice to embody the best of that humanity through the compassionate actions we display toward each other every day. This book has been a manual for making that choice operational.

We began with the word "vagina" and its etymology as a "sheath" — an accessory to be filled. We end with the word "consent" and its etymology from consentire — "to feel together." That is the journey of this entire book. From accessory to agency. From sheath to sovereign territory. From silence to shared sensation.

Consent is not a contract signed in triplicate. It is not a legal disclaimer. It is a shared sensation — a moment in which two human beings have agreed to exist in the same reality, with the same enthusiasm.

I do not harbor resentment or hatred toward the sword. I love men. I love the energy they bring to our shared humanity and our shared sexuality. My mission has always been to raise awareness that the scabbard is not an inanimate object. It is a person. It is a sovereign territory with its own borders, its own right to self-governance, and its own right to say, "Not today."

What we are doing is building a Village Firewall. We are turning whispers into roars. We are empowering our officers, engaging our fathers, resetting our codes, and installing antivirus in every community that will have us.

The operating system is ready. It is safer. It is more profitable. And if we do this right, it will be a lot more fun.

Have more safety.

Have more sex.

Have more space.

Welcome to:

"The more beautiful world our hearts know is possible."
— Charles Eisenstein

GLOSSARY OF CODES & CONCEPTS

For the sake of clarity, every code in this book derives its uniqueness from its own command, which could be any one, or a combination of, these three:

DELETE - Malware to remove

EDIT - Scripts to rewrite

SAVE - New code to install

This glossary is your personal library, and it will serve as a mini-dictionary to help you understand the specific codes and ideas for our new consent culture without interrupting your flow of reading and grasp of the new language. These are the codes you have learned across the fourteen chapters of the book. Possess them. Own them. Carry them.

Accountability Gap [DELETE]

The distance between knowing and acting. When multiple people are aware of a problem and no one acts on that knowledge. The gap widens over time and cost compounds; financial, human, and institutional. The gap is not ignorance. It is architecture.

The Accountability Gap does not close itself. It closes when leaders decide to close it.

CHAPTER 12 — THE ACCOUNTABILITY GAP

Agency Code [SAVE]

The shift from exploitation code to ownership code. The person on the screen controls the channel, the content, and the consent. The creator economy has removed the middleman and put boundary-setting power back in the performer's hands. Regardless of moral stance on the content, the consent architecture has improved.

When a woman owns the channel, she owns the consent.

CHAPTER 6 — THE TRAGIC MYSTIQUE OF PORN

Bystander Code (5 D's) [SAVE]

Framework for intervening when witnessing potential harm. Originally developed by Green Dot, expanded by Right To Be. Five options at every comfort level: Direct (confront), Distract (interrupt the dynamic), Delegate (bring in backup), Delay (check in after), Document (record what you see). Trainable, certifiable, and practicable.

Curiosity is a superpower. When something feels off, get curious.

CHAPTER 11 — THE MISSING CODE

Carbon Copy [DELETE]

Any behavior you replicate without conscious choice. Scripts installed by family, culture, peers, media, and fear. The "uncle hug" you perform on autopilot. The automatic "yes" when your gut says "no." The silence when someone makes your skin crawl. These are not choices. They are copies.

You are not broken. You were just running someone else's code.

CHAPTER 3 — DEFINING THE CONSENT CODE

Carbon Copy Scan [SAVE]

The practice of making one unconscious behavior conscious per week. Pick one. Pause before reacting. Ask: "Did I choose this, or did I copy it?" If you copied it, run the debugger. Train it like checking your blind spot; repetition until the conscious choice becomes the default.

Name it. Scan it. Decide if it stays or goes.

CHAPTER 14 — THE NEW CODE

Check-In Ritual [SAVE]

Two words: "Still good?" Built into the sequence until skipping them feels as wrong as driving unbuckled. Applies in the bedroom, at a party, in a meeting, at the dinner table. Consent is not the brakes. It is the engine.

Two words. Infinite applications.

CHAPTER 14 — THE NEW CODE

Coercive Control [DELETE]

One of the two malware codes identified in the Four CCs. Coercive Control is the virus — behavior that seeks to dominate, often without lifting a finger. Legally defined under 22 U.S.C. § 7102 (Trafficking Victims Protection

Act), coercion includes threats of serious harm, abuse of the legal process, or schemes intended to cause a person to believe they will be harmed if they don't comply. Restraint is not required. If your reputation has been threatened, that is coercion. If you have been subjected to financial manipulation, that is coercion. If you have been so isolated that you feel you have no exit, that is coercion. The law validates what your intuition has known all along.

If you felt forced, you were forced.

CHAPTER 3 — DEFINING THE CONSENT CODE

Community Care Code [SAVE]

Shame never belonged to the survivor. This code moves it where it belongs — onto the community to support, and onto the system to hold the perpetrator accountable. Community Care is the distributed security system: when everyone runs the same antivirus, the predator can't find a host. It lives in the questions we ask, the check-ins we build into our rituals, the protective function we carry and extend — with tech or without it. The antidote to victim blaming is curiosity.

When someone picks up the courage to tell you, refuse to jump onto a judgmental platform. Wake up your curiosity.

CHAPTER 7 — THE COERCIVE PREDATOR

Consent Code [SAVE]

From the Latin consentire: "to feel together." The shared understanding and active agreement between individuals created through transparency, communication, and respect for boundaries; with the freedom to say "no" without consequence. Not a contract. A shared sensation.

Consent is not a contract signed in triplicate. It is a moment in which two human beings have agreed to exist in the same reality, with the same enthusiasm.

CHAPTER 3 — DEFINING THE CONSENT CODE

DARVO [DELETE]

Deny, Attack, Reverse Victim and Offender. This is the predictable sequence that institutions and perpetrators use to deflect accountability. Deny ("That never happened"), Attack ("She's unstable"), Reverse ("We're the real victims here"). It runs identically at the individual and institutional level.

The pattern is so reliable you can set your watch by it.

CHAPTER 12 — THE ACCOUNTABILITY GAP

Delete. Edit. Save. [SAVE]

This is the core debugger sequence of the entire book. Three commands applied to communities, culture, and connections. DELETE the malware — shame scripts, obligation scripts, the Perfect Victim checklist. EDIT the question — from "Why did you go there?" to "Who did this?" SAVE the new default — boundaries that honor your gut, laws that ask "Did she agree?"

The framework is simple: three commands. Delete code. Edit code. Save code. Apply them to our communities, our culture, and our connections, and human kindness becomes the default setting.

INTRODUCTION — APPLIED THROUGHOUT

The Digital Blame Code [DELETE]

Same script, new platform. The question used to be "Why did you walk down that road?" Now it is "Why did you send that photo?" and "Why did you give him your number?" Consent given in one context does not transfer to another. A photo shared privately is not permission to distribute.

Delete 'Why did you send that photo?' Replace: 'Why did he share it without consent?'

CHAPTER 4 — THE SHAME CODE

Docile Code — Friction [DELETE — SAVE]

The Docile Code says: "Don't make it awkward, don't intrude, don't stay too long." The predator counts on it. Friction is the replacement: connection, presence, awareness. Stay. Use names. Check in. Be awkward. Intrude a little. None of this requires spotting a predator. It just requires stopping the Docile Code.

Be awkward. Intrude a little. Stay.

CHAPTER 7 — THE COERCIVE PREDATOR

Enter and Exit Framework [SAVE]

Every interaction has an entrance and an exit. Explicitly open the container: name what you want and what you need. Explicitly close it: name where you are and what comes next. When the exit is visible, people stop scanning for danger and show up with their full attention.

You cannot feel safe in a room if the door is locked from the outside.

CHAPTER 14 — THE NEW CODE

Enthusiasm Over Control [SAVE]

The core distinction between healthy desire and predatory behavior. The Playboy Code needs enthusiasm to feel satisfied. The Predator Code needs control. One lives on mutual pleasure. The other gets off on dominance. The test is simple: "Do you need your partner's enthusiasm, or do you need their compliance?"

One code runs on mutual fire. The other runs on someone else's silence.

CHAPTER 5 — THE TOURIST
CHAPTER 7 - THE COERCIVE PREDATOR

Galloway's Moral Infrastructure for Young Men [SAVE]

Scott Galloway's framework: Young men need Structure (where to put their energy), Ritual (practices that build identity and belonging), and Challenge (tests that prove capability). When society eliminates these without a replacement, dark substitutes fill the void.

Young men need structure. They need ritual. They need challenge. When we take those away without replacement, we don't get healthier men — we get lost ones.

CHAPTER 11 — THE MISSING CODE

Honest Itinerary [SAVE]

A pre-encounter self-assessment. Three questions answered before your next encounter: What am I actually offering? (Residency, a visit, one night, exploration.) What do I actually want? Am I willing to say this honestly to the other person? Transparency is the operating system. If you cannot answer these out loud, you are not ready to engage.

The problem was never tourism. The problem was lying about the itinerary.

CHAPTER 5 — THE TOURIST

Human Mycelium [SAVE]

The distributed infrastructure underneath the Queen Code. Like mycelium — the fungal threads connecting trees underground, exchanging nutrients and warnings across entire forests — women are building digital root systems that share data instantly. Touch one node, activate the entire system. The predator's vulnerability scan was built for isolated targets. When the network is connected, no one is truly alone. The scan returns zero reliable results. The code is obsolete.

Touch one node, activate the entire system.

CHAPTER 7 — THE COERCIVE PREDATOR

Institutional Betrayal [DELETE]

When an institution fails the very people it exists to protect. Ignoring reports, silencing survivors, prioritizing reputation or capitalism over truth and human kindness. The betrayal compounds the original trauma; the survivor is harmed by the perpetrator and by the system that was supposed to help.

The institution that should protect you becomes the second wound.

CHAPTER 12 — THE ACCOUNTABILITY GAP

Institutional Courage [SAVE]

Dr. Jennifer Freyd's framework for an institution's commitment to seek truth and engage in moral action despite unpleasantness, risk, and short-term cost. Compliance is the floor, not the ceiling. Twelve operationalized steps from baseline legal compliance to cherishing whistleblowers and addressing root causes.

Are we building compliance or courage?

CHAPTER 12 — THE ACCOUNTABILITY GAP

Label Machine [DELETE]

A 500-year-old algorithm that automatically converts "Woman Challenging Power" into "Discredited Object." Select from: Witch, Whore, Crazy, Liar, Gold Digger. Apply label. Execute credibility destruction. Output: "She is the problem." The labels function. They do not describe.

The stake burned bodies. Servers burn reputations. Same operating system.

CHAPTER 9 — WITCHES OF THE PAST; WHORES OF TODAY

Label Translator [EDIT]

The translation layer that installs a pause between hearing a label and reacting to it. When you hear "Gold digger," ask "What is she actually owed?" When you hear "Crazy," ask "What behavior prompted this label?" When you hear "Liar," ask "What evidence exists either way?"

The label is a weapon, not a descriptor.

CHAPTER 9 — WITCHES OF THE PAST, WHORES OF TODAY

Legacy Code (Law Enforcement) [DELETE]

The default operating system in American policing that prioritizes control, compliance, and dominance over communication and consent negotiation. Sixty hours of firearm training versus eight hours of de-escalation. Officers equipped to escalate, not communicate. Warriors trained, Protectors needed.

We train officers to win fights. We don't train them to prevent fights. That's the gap.

CHAPTER 10 — THE DISARMED OFFICE

Man Code [SAVE]

If you are a father of daughters, you feel this in your bones, but fatherhood is not the prerequisite. This is not a Dad Code. It is a Man Code. Every man has a front door. Protection extends from that door outward. If you are not a dad, consider the uncle role, the brother role, the coach role. The decision that "not her" means "not anyone."

Your protection does not stop at your front door.

CHAPTER 14 — THE NEW CODE

The Perfect Victim Checklist [DELETE]

The legal system's impossible checklist. Was she sober? Did she physically fight back? Does she have a clean sexual history? Did she report immediately? Is there physical evidence? If all checks pass, process the case. If any check fails, default to blame.

The Perfect Victim does not exist. That is the point.

CHAPTER 4 — THE SHAME CODE

Proactive Duty [SAVE]

The emerging legal standard requiring employers to prevent harassment rather than just respond after it occurs. The UK Worker Protection Act 2023 mandates "reasonable steps" to prevent. California requires written Workplace Violence Prevention Plans. The paradigm shift: from "Who did this?" to "Why did the system allow this?"

The law is moving toward prevention. Move with it or be left behind.

CHAPTER 12 — THE ACCOUNTABILITY GAP

Queen Code [SAVE]

The personal decision to plug into the distributed protection network women are already running. Every woman who chooses — individually, autonomously — to share what she knows activates the system. The Queen Code is not about the network itself. It is about the choice to stop keeping what you know to yourself and to share the data that keeps other women safe, even when the old code tells you to stay quiet, mind your business, or worry about being called "dramatic." Not a whisper network born of fear; a Village Firewall built out of abundance. Protected by Truth Defense and Anti-SLAPP laws. Every time one woman plugs in, the entire system gets stronger.

You do not need permission to activate your Queen Code. You just need the decision that silence is no longer the default.

CHAPTER 7 — THE COERCIVE PREDATOR / CHAPTER 14 — THE NEW CODE

Resident vs. Tourist [SAVE]

Two valid relationship operating systems. The Resident commits, buys property, invests in long-term infrastructure. The Tourist visits with great energy, appreciates the destination, and does not pretend that the trip is permanent. Both are valid. Neither is deception. Violation only occurs when a Tourist pretends to be a Resident.

The Tourist cleans up after themselves and leaves the destination better than they found it.

CHAPTER 5 — THE TOURIST

The Shame Code [DELETE]

The victim-blaming script that runs automatically after assault, producing silence as its output. Shame leads to self-blame leads to "Will anyone believe me?" (returns false) leads to "Will reporting make it worse?" (returns true) leads to silence. Designed by a system that shifts blame from predator to victim.

This was never your code to carry.

CHAPTER 4 — THE SHAME CODE

Signal (One, Two, Three) [SAVE]

Nonverbal consent visibility. One finger = Red (No/Stop). Two fingers = Yellow (Pause/I need to talk). Three fingers = Green (Yes/Go ahead). No speech required. Removes the verbal barrier. Available as an app.

If the Consent Code is the software, this is one of the simplest pieces of hardware to run it on.

CHAPTER 14 — THE NEW CODE

Silence Code [DELETE]

The operational invisibility that allows predators to function at scale. Each victim believes she is alone. Mega-cases take decades to surface because no one connects the dots. Every predator runs the same calculation: If I stay invisible, I stay operational. Technology is deleting this variable.

The predator's greatest asset is not strength. It is darkness.

CHAPTER 7 — THE COERCIVE PREDATOR

Terminology Upgrade Menu [EDIT]

Language is the first line of code. The "Playboy" archetype signals agency — *I chose this.* Historical female equivalents signal passivity — *this happened to me.* DELETE the shame vocabulary: Slut, Loose, Easy, Whore, Player. UPGRADE to terms that honor choice, philosophy, and ownership of sexuality without shame: The Libertine. The Bon Vivant. The Sovereign. The Free Agent. The Pleasure Activist. The Tourist.

The language you use installs the code you run.

CHAPTER 5 — THE TOURIST

Three-Stage Consent Education [SAVE]

HMS framework for training institutions. Stage 1: Recognition (identifying when consent is absent). Stage 2: Response (trauma-informed communication, de-escalation). Stage 3: Reporting (accurate documentation, victim-centered process).

When you train people, fund programs, and create expectation of intervention, people intervene.

CHAPTER 10 — THE DISARMED OFFICE

Vetting Void [DELETE]

The systemic failure to conduct basic due diligence before appointments, promotions, or partnerships. Not because information is unavailable, but because systems do not prioritize looking. If a basic docket search would reveal the problem, conduct the search.

Everyone asks "How did no one know?" They could have known. They didn't look.

CHAPTER 12 — THE ACCOUNTABILITY GAP

Viewer's Vote [SAVE]

Delete/Edit/Save applied to media consumption. DELETE shows using sexual violence as default drama. EDIT by naming the manipulation: "That's Old Code." SAVE the evolved stories; shows that hire Intimacy Coordinators, narratives built on connection and agency. The industry follows the audience.

If a show hooks you with lazy trauma porn in the first ten minutes, turn it off.

CHAPTER 6 — THE TRAGIC MYSTIQUE OF PORN

Visual Hijacking [DELETE]

The neurological rewiring that occurs when heavy porn consumption trains the brain to respond primarily to visual stimuli rather than physical sensation, emotional connection, or real-world arousal cues. Porn acts as a supranormal stimulus delivering unnaturally high dopamine surges that real-life encounters rarely match.

The screen trains the brain to need what the body was never designed to require.

CHAPTER 6 — THE TRAGIC MYSTIQUE OF PORN

Vulnerability Scan [DELETE]

The subconscious algorithm predators run to identify targets. Not random; systematic assessment of gait, posture, and boundary response. Ninety percent agreement among offenders on who is vulnerable, based solely on watching people walk. The scan fails against those who are embodied, alert, and connected.

It is a sharable scanning code — and it fails against those who are embodied, alert, and connected.

CHAPTER 7 — THE COERCIVE PREDATOR